LEGAL PRACTIC

PERSONAL
MANAGEMENT SKILLS

LEGAL PRACTICE HANDBOOK

PERSONAL MANAGEMENT SKILLS

Stephen W. Mayson, LLB, LLM, Barrister
Managing Partner, Hildebrandt, London
Visiting Professor of International Legal Practice,
Nottingham Law School

Series Editor: Anthony G. King, MA, Solicitor
Director of Education, Clifford Chance

BLACKSTONE
PRESS LIMITED

First published in Great Britain 1992 by Blackstone Press Limited,
9–15 Aldine Street, London W12 8AW. Telephone 081–740 1173

ISBN: 1 85431 166 2

British Library Cataloguing in Publication Data
A CIP catalogue record for this book is available from the British
Library

Typeset by Style Photosetting Ltd, Mayfield, East Sussex
Printed by BPCC Wheatons Ltd, Exeter

Contents

Preface

Writing about professional skills forces one to face up to a dilemma. Many of the precepts in this book will be obvious to any lawyer with any degree of practical experience. For the novice practitioner, much of the detail will at first sight appear irrelevant or assume a greater degree of influence over his or her working environment than reality permits. I make no apology for stating the obvious, for it is so often the common-sense approach to practice that is overlooked in the hurly-burly of a busy professional life. If all I do is bring together within these covers a structured collection and exposition of common-sense practice, I regard that as valuable.

The book is directed towards trainee solicitors and the recently qualified. I know from experience that two-year qualified solicitors and beyond display a degree of cynicism about learning (or even discussing) these supposedly 'basic' skills, but I believe that even experienced practitioners will benefit from reviewing their working habits.

The principal messages of the text are:

(a)   The value of the period of articles has been eroded over the years because of pressure to deal more quickly with complex and specialised matters, and to produce fee income as soon as possible. As a result, greater efforts must be made to develop formally professional skills that have traditionally been imbued by sharing space, time and experience with senior lawyers.

(b)   Try to adopt the habit of looking at all your professional actions from the client's point of view.

(c)   Waste no opportunity to learn – even if only by observing more experienced lawyers in the pursuance of their craft.

I should like to thank the many firms and lawyers who have allowed me over the years to observe them, and to train them, in the performance of the skills discussed in this book. Their contribution is apparent on every page. I must also thank my partner, Joel Henning, and the series editor, Tony King, for their valuable insights and comments on the original manuscript. Needless to say, responsibility for the final product is entirely mine.

Stephen Mayson
Chancery House
Chancery Lane
London WC2

Introduction

Learning by Doing

This book is for all practitioners, whether in large firms or small, in contentious work or non-contentious, in cities or rural areas, in firms focused mainly on private client work, commercial work, or a mixture of both. It is written primarily for trainee solicitors and other junior lawyers, though it may profitably be read by even the most seasoned practitioners. (Those tempted to consider themselves beyond the ambit of the messages in the pages that follow should perhaps start at appendix 3 and then, with their minds hopefully refocused, return to this introduction!)

The transition from law school to law office can be daunting and frustrating. Trained over a period of four years or more to recognise legal issues that come packaged in half a page by examiners is often not adequate preparation for the rough and tumble of the real world. Worse than that, in commercial law firms, the type of law practised often bears little relation to the academic or vocational subjects you have been taught. A diet of Eurobond financing, tax structuring, flotations, aircraft leasing and the like is not staple fare for the average law student (nor even for the average lawyer, to be fair). The day-to-day reality of dealing with live clients who bring relatively straightforward domestic or commercial problems is sufficient to throw many would-be practitioners into a state of panic. Coping with this and the sheer novelty of working within what should be a business organisation represents a time of great challenge (and strain) for most young lawyers.

The period of training immediately following law school is all about learning by doing. Historically, the period of articles has always been seen in this light. But when the notion of articles was conceived, the law was less complex and less specialised, clients less demanding, competition less intense, and there was a real opportunity to sit with one's principal and learn by example and discussion. The pressure of modern legal practice rarely gives the opportunity for this more leisurely approach to learning the art of the legal practitioner. Further, the sophistication of client work often produces less of the small type of transactions on which trainees can cut their teeth.

In these circumstances, learning by doing becomes a different proposition. At worst, the whole process is one of osmosis – and the trouble with that is that you are just as likely to pick up bad techniques and habits as good ones. The 'sink or swim' mentality is firmly engrained in the culture of many law firms (since that is the way most of the senior lawyers learned their craft), but it does not recognise how much the practice of law has changed – and practitioners along with it.

Whatever happens, there is no substitute for learning by doing, and no other way of becoming an effective lawyer. However, completely unstructured and untutored learning benefits no one. There is now greater recognition that being a good lawyer involves a wide range of skills and abilities, and none of them are innate.

In today's increasingly competitive environment, more than ever before, the need to be professional in your dealings with clients is vital. Being professional is a combination of many things, but principally involves 'going the extra mile' for your clients, truly caring for clients, and being organised to provide the most efficient service you can – being on time, not keeping people waiting, responding to letters, telephone calls and requests within the shortest time possible. Professionalism has little to do with the law itself, but everything to do with the conduct and behaviour of lawyers towards their clients, other professionals, colleagues and staff, and towards each other.

This book is part of a series designed to raise your awareness and interest in the skills required. Just as you cannot learn to ride a bicycle or to play golf by reading, so you will not acquire your lawyer's skills by reading about them. But you will acquire a more formal structure within which to assimilate and assess the skills you need and that you see demonstrated by all other lawyers day by day.

Make the most of every opportunity you are given to develop new skills and to practise them. Create opportunities where they do not otherwise exist. Never lose your thirst for improvement and development, and do not accept less than the highest quality of work and service from yourself. Only in this way will you develop into a first-rate practitioner. Only in this way is the legal profession certain of a secure future.

Every law firm is different – sometimes in subtle ways, sometimes in strikingly obvious ways. Not only that, every practitioner is also different. A book such as this cannot therefore be prescriptive or didactic. It can only give ideas and suggestions based on experience of a wide range of lawyers and law firms. The following pages should be read on that basis. At different stages of your career, new responsibilities will be given to you which will require changes in the way you work and in the skills you use. In some firms, those responsibilities will come earlier than they will in others. Accordingly, the description of the range of skills dealt with in this book will vary from individual to individual, and from time to time. Your ability to influence those around you will also vary. If the skills or solutions described here do not seem immediately appropriate, do not dismiss them: think ahead – they may be needed or be possible tomorrow, next week, next month, next year, or in your next firm!

Chapter One

Teamwork

1.1 INTRODUCTION

Having spent a number of years working on your own in the pursuit of education and qualifications, one of the greatest shocks awaiting you as a young practitioner is the reliance you now have to place on other people. Not only that, but as the smallest cog in the wheel, your ability to influence the actions and decisions of those around you is very limited. You are now responsible to others for what you do, when you do it, and how you do it. Although you may not realise it, or be made to feel like it, you are now part of a team.

1.2 UNDERSTANDING YOUR ROLE

This is difficult. Your role will vary depending on which firm you are in; what size it is; where it is; if there are specialisations, which department you are in; what sort of law you are practising; who you work with; and what stage you have reached in your career.

Suffice it to say, however, that in the early days your role will be limited. Some firms will regard you as a trainee, willing to spend time and effort training you to handle the different components of your work, developing the new expertise and skills you need. Others will regard you as a fee-earning resource whose job it is to generate a return on the salary and associated costs of having you around. You can learn a lot from both situations, but you need more initiative and resilience to cope with the latter.

In short, your role is to develop into an effective, practising lawyer as quickly as possible. You must do whatever is expected of you with good grace and enthusiasm (assuming it is legal, decent, honest and ethical). Take advantage of any formal training you are offered, and do not take too narrow a view of what is 'relevant' to your future needs. The recession of the early 1990s has left many specialists wishing they had taken a wider interest in what was going on in other parts of the firm or the profession.

It is the essence of being a team member that you do not work alone. There must be leaders (usually partners), providing work, supervision and motivation; there must be workers (usually other qualified lawyers); and there needs to be support (in the form of secretaries and other administrative and support staff). Last, but certainly not least, there must be clients. We will examine these elements in this chapter.

1.3 DELEGATION AND SUPERVISION

Whatever formal training you have had, and however good it was, none of it will have prepared you for the real world. There is no substitute for on-the-job training. Your professional development truly begins when you start working on a real matter for a real client. But unstructured and unsupervised training is no good for anyone, so the value of your on-the-job training will depend in large measure on the quality of the delegation and supervision you receive. We will look in this section at the process of delegation, and the roles of the supervisor and the supervised.

1.3.1 The process of delegation

To some, delegation means the abdication of responsibility for something, a giving away. They are not good delegators, and rarely work well with others. What they overlook is that delegation also involves an assumption of responsibility – the responsibility of supervision, involving explanation, discussion and training (see

1.3.2). The professional responsibility to a client can never be abdicated.

There are others who believe that delegation is a waste of time because it is always quicker for them to do things themselves and they will always do a better job. These people are misguided, and have usually forgotten their own tentative and nervous beginnings. It should be inevitable that they would carry out work more quickly and to a higher standard than someone who is learning. However, if they never give younger lawyers the opportunity to develop, they waste the firm's investment in new people. Not only that, but they will also condemn themselves to the same type and standard of work because they are denying themselves the time to develop their own expertise and experience. Further, since senior lawyers generally cost more than junior ones, they may be costing the client more money for a higher level of service than the client really needs, wants or expects to pay for.

The most effective way of working is to delegate work down to the lowest competent level at which it can be handled. Unless this happens, the time and expertise of senior people is often wasted doing things that can perfectly well be done by others; more senior or sophisticated tasks are not tackled; and the talent of more junior people is never sufficiently developed or groomed for senior and more challenging roles. Failing to delegate is ultimately a recipe for professional stagnation.

It may be some time before you are the delegator, but do consider and observe early in your career the skills and attitudes needed by those in 'leadership' positions.

When you are in a position to delegate, you should consider:

   (a)   What is the job that is to be delegated? Sometimes this might be the whole of a matter or task, sometimes just part of a larger project or matter. Whatever it is, you should be quite clear about the extent of the work you are delegating and the implications for the recipient. If you are not delegating an entire project, try to explain the wider picture so that the recipient sees the implications of his or her work and input. Do not regard delegation as an opportunity to palm off matters or tasks that you have no interest in.

(b) Who has the skills to perform the job – or who could develop the skills under supervision? Gaining experience in different areas is an important part of the overall professional development of most lawyers. When such matters become available, it is therefore important that you think about involving a lawyer who could benefit from the challenge of a new assignment. There is a real danger in having lawyers who are known for doing certain types of work or for having a particular expertise, because they are likely always to be given work of that type or calling for that expertise. A fine balance needs to be maintained. Of course it makes sense to use experienced practitioners for new client work, but a firm should also make sure that it does not shunt its emerging talent into a premature and narrow siding.

(c) Who is available? In a busy law firm, it may frequently happen that a lawyer whom you would like to involve in a new matter is tied up with other client work. In any event, the way you allocate new work must take account of existing work distribution within your department or within the firm so that certain lawyers are not overloaded, and that the development opportunities described above can be realised. These are management issues, but they affect all lawyers in a firm and, ultimately, the quality of the service experienced by clients.

Delegation is not simply a process of handing over a file or a task with a perfunctory injunction to 'Get back to me as soon as possible' (though you will be lucky to go through the early years of your career without being the victim of this approach at least once). As a good delegator you will spend time supervising the whole job from start to finish (in fact, the expressions 'delegator' and 'supervisor' are interchangeable, since you cannot delegate without supervising). Let us examine next the elements of considerate delegation and supervision.

1.3.2 The role of the supervisor

A good supervisor will do a number of things:

(a) Make a commitment: commit yourself to the process of delegation and supervision, to making time for the person being supervised, and to being accessible.

(b)   Give clear and specific assignments: indicate what must be done, by when, and in what form (e.g., draft letter or other document, research note, oral report). If appropriate, you may indicate how the work should be undertaken, what sources might be used, who could be spoken to, and how much time should be spent on the various tasks or components of the matter. The best supervisors also back up their delegation of a matter with a written assignment form or memorandum, and indicate at what intervals they expect feedback. This will depend on your own preferences, the nature of your practice, and the culture of the firm, but should not be dismissed too quickly as an unnecessary piece of administration.

(c)   Monitor the work being done and the progress being made: be quite clear about when you expect progress reports or feedback. Not only that, but keep the supervisee and other people who are working with you informed about what is going on.

(d)   Provide feedback on performance: this is the part that many lawyers find the most difficult. Trained to be hypercritical, and to pick holes in the work of others, lawyers are often too easily tempted to adopt the same style as a training method. Criticism may be necessary, but it should always be done in private, and accompanied by positive reinforcement. The feedback you give must be constructive, otherwise the learning value of the assignment will be lost. The first step in this process is for you to accept the concepts of error, failure or loss: those being supervised will never produce work in the same way or of the same quality that you would, partly because they are not as skilled as you and partly because everyone is different in their style or approach. If you rewrite a piece of work, explain why. Stylistic differences only should never be criticised, though better ways of doing or saying things should be pointed out. Remember when you delegate something that it will often be because the client does not need (or cannot afford) your level of service and quality. Do not therefore expect the person to whom you delegate to perform to your standard. Your objective is to get the work done – but not by you. Provided the work produced reaches an acceptable level of competence and quality for the job in hand, you will have achieved your objective.

1.3.3 The role of the supervised

The days of delegating may seem some way off, but part of the success of a delegator lies in having been an active and thoughtful recipient of delegated work.

If all supervisors were good at delegation and supervision, the role of the supervised would be much easier. However, you will experience many differences in style and ability (all of which you should bear in mind when you are in a position to supervise others).

With each assignment, you should:

(a) Be sure you know what you have been assigned to do – what the limits of your brief and authority are, the time-scale involved (including any deadlines or time-limits), and the form of the response you are expected to make (there is no point preparing a 50-page research note if the matter partner is expecting a five-minute verbal report). After due consideration, if you are not sure how to go about the assigned task, or how much time you should be spending on it, ask for guidance. Better that than waste time and effort doing things that are not required or are leading up the wrong alley.

(b) Establish how often and when you are expected to report back: this should always be done on a regular basis, even if you have not yet completed the task that was given to you. In this way, both you and your supervisor can discuss whether you are on the right track without either of you becoming disillusioned or disappointed.

(c) Seek feedback on your work. However the feedback is expressed, try to look for the positive comments that you can learn from. Accept that you will make mistakes, and that sometimes you may miss the point completely. Try not to take criticism personally (even though it will often feel very personal). And when a draft document that you have spent many hours putting together is returned to you unrecognisable and indistinguishable from the red ink of your supervisor, try to learn from the substantive corrections (hopefully your supervisor will discuss these with you, but do not be afraid to ask for enlightenment) and try not to be offended by the stylistic changes. Some supervisors adopt a crusading approach to correcting writing style. If you have been asked to draft a letter or other document on behalf of your supervisor, this is fair enough – it is your supervisor's document and should read as if he or she had written it. If the document is yours, you must certainly listen to the comments that are made, but if they are purely stylistic and you are not convinced of the merit of any suggested changes, grit your teeth and continue to develop your own style elsewhere.

A problem faced by many younger lawyers is obtaining feedback on work they have done for more senior partners who are (or appear to be) too busy or unapproachable to talk to. The first thing to remember is that it was the senior lawyer who gave the work out in the first place. Their priorities will change, often at very short notice, and so persistence will usually be required. If you know from experience that a particular lawyer is difficult to get hold of, do not leave feedback until the last moment – build in some time to allow for slippage against deadlines.

If what you need is not so much guidance in handling the work but more an appraisal of your performance, persistence is likewise required, though you may find some senior lawyers less willing to participate. Some older lawyers are reluctant to invest the time or the effort in this process, or are simply too uncomfortable or embarrassed to make it work effectively. In these circumstances, talk to another appropriate partner, such as your principal, the partner responsible for trainee solicitors, the personnel or training partner, or someone else who is willing to talk to you about your progress. Law firms are notorious for adopting the 'sink or swim' approach, and you must find your own buoyancy aids wherever you can.

1.4 LEADERSHIP

Much research has been conducted into leadership. It is exercised in many different contexts and with many different styles. There is no right way to do it. The leadership skills and styles of the armed forces or of captains of industry are not necessarily suitable in a modern law firm. Leadership is certainly required, but this is not the place to debate its meaning.

The most potent and effective leadership anywhere is leadership by example. In a law firm, this usually means the leadership of partners, but, in the eyes of secretarial and support staff, it may mean the behaviour of all lawyers. For example, if partners and senior lawyers do not return all telephone calls to clients promptly, it is unlikely that anyone will. If partners do not follow office procedures, there is no incentive or role model to persuade anyone else to. If partners keep untidy offices, they are sending a message that such disorganisation is acceptable throughout the firm. If lawyers go around grumbling about clients, the odds are that something of this feeling will reflect in the way secretaries react to clients.

Although as a trainee solicitor or junior lawyer you may not feel like a leader, in your professional behaviour start as you mean to go on. Many law firms suffer from divisions between their lawyers and non-lawyers – secretarial and administrative staff are regarded as lesser human beings. Such treatment of others is unforgivable and unprofessional. Treat everyone as no less than your equal in human terms (of course, professionally they may be much more than your equal, but that does not alter their humanity). Poor staff relations do not have to remain a self-fulfilling prophesy in law firms.

1.5 MOTIVATION

As with leadership, much research has been conducted into what motivates people. Not surprisingly, there are wide divergences, though some common threads seem to exist. Again, this is not the place to debate any general theories of motivation, but a few observations are worth making.

In broad terms, most career-minded lawyers are self-motivated individuals. This means that there is often little that can be done directly to increase their motivation, though quite a lot can be done that will demotivate them. For example, if partners keep quality work to themselves, or behave in a condescending, critical manner towards their assistant solicitors, those solicitors are likely to be demotivated. Similarly, other things being equal, money will not positively motivate, though lack of it (or, more often, perceived unfair differentials between individuals) will demotivate. The challenge for law firm leaders, therefore, is not so much to find ways of motivating lawyers as to create an environment in which their self-motivation can flourish, and in which they do not become demotivated.

Non-lawyers are likely to be motivated by other things, and more traditional approaches to reward and motivation may need to be adopted. Every lawyer needs to bear this in mind, not just the partners. You cannot treat secretarial and support staff as if they are motivated in the same ways that you are and as if they had the same single-minded devotion to furthering their own careers as you do.

1.6   SECRETARIAL AND SUPPORT STAFF

When most lawyers think of teamwork, they think of the work they do with other lawyers in the firm. But the production of professional work is the result of teamwork with others as well. Little of your work might see life outside the firm were it not for the cooperation and support of your secretary. Teamwork with a secretary is considered in detail in chapter 4.

Similarly, teamwork between lawyers, secretaries and other support staff is necessary. Today's law firm is a complex and, in many cases, multimillion-pound business. Whilst lawyers tend to affect a professional disdain for things administrative, the truth is that those lawyers could not perform effectively without administrative support. The 'us and them' gulf already referred to between lawyers and non-lawyers conspires against teamwork. Indeed, a direct result may be administrators believing that their work exists in its own right, in isolation from legal work – leading to self-fulfilling bureaucracy so despised by practising lawyers. Cooperation and communication are necessary for lawyers to work efficiently, for administrators to perform properly and economically, and for clients to be served better by your firm than by your competitors.

1.7   CLIENTS

Before we leave teamwork, let us not forget that clients are now better educated and more sophisticated than ever. Most of them know what they want to achieve and what to expect from their lawyers. The best way to serve clients is not to take instructions, do the work, and send them a bill, but to regard the client as part of the team with you so that you work together to achieve the result the client wants. Indeed, in commercial work, many corporate clients have their own in-house lawyers who may well lead the 'team' of in-house and external lawyers, and require you to play the role assigned by them.

Clients also tend not to be too impressed with lawyers who pick fights with lawyers acting for other parties – even in contentious matters. Assertion and vigorous representation have their place, but not all matters are antagonistic, and many require a team effort from all involved.

1.8   SUMMARY OF KEY ISSUES

(a)   Teamwork from everyone is vital to the efficient delivery of legal services, the satisfaction of clients' needs, and the profitable practice of law.

(b)   Your initial role may be limited, but it is up to you to take advantage of all opportunities you are given to develop your skills and knowledge.

(c)   Delegation is critical to the development of individual lawyers and to the firm as a whole. The work to be delegated should be defined, the required skills identified, and availability determined.

(d)   A good supervisor will make a commitment to the process of delegation, give clear and specific assignments, and provide constructive feedback.

(e)   A good supervisee will also make a commitment to work from a clear understanding of what is required, and will report back regularly.

(f)   The leadership of professional people is based on example and mutual respect, and involves creating an environment that motivates (or at least does not demotivate) intelligent and independently minded people.

Chapter Two

Meetings

2.1 INTRODUCTION

Lawyers are notorious for spending time in meetings. Almost every time a client calls, a secretary explains that the lawyer 'is in a meeting'. When the lawyer comes out of the meeting, invariably it is described as 'a waste of time'. Nevertheless, meetings are an important and inevitable part of professional life, and with a little forethought can become more productive if not more enjoyable.

Compared with many more formal types of meetings, most of the meetings that lawyers are involved in are inherently less structured. Often, there is a series of meetings moving towards some desired end for the client's benefit. Nevertheless, all meetings have objectives and can be more structured. Too frequently, these objectives and opportunities for structure go unstated or even unthought-of.

In this chapter, we shall be looking principally at how meetings can be made more productive. We shall concentrate on meetings held for some client-related purpose, whether they involve clients and lawyers, lawyers and other advisers, or just lawyers. The principles apply equally well, however, to other meetings, including internal gatherings.

When you first attend meetings, you will probably find that you are a 'passive' participant. For this reason, parts of this chapter might also seem passive. However, use the opportunity of going to meetings to observe and learn from what others do – assess what works and what does not, and the circumstances in which some meetings are more successful and productive than others.

2.2 A DEFINITION

The first (and major) key to effective meetings is to understand what they truly are. During the course of every working day you will talk to people who walk into your office or who you meet in the corridors. Although you are, in a sense, meeting people, these encounters are not 'meetings' for our purposes. There are four principal elements we need to consider: organisation, purpose, communication and relevance.

2.2.1 Organisation

Since meetings proper are not just chance encounters, they must be organised to bring two or more people together in the same place at the same time. Trying to find a time when busy people can meet together can be a difficult task in itself, and the logistics of doing so should not be underestimated.

In many firms, these logistics will be undertaken by the secretary of the lawyer responsible for calling the meeting. On some occasions, however, the task will fall to you. The following is a checklist of (self-evident) factors that need to be considered:

(a) Arrange a time convenient to everyone: two major factors of 'convenience' is where a meeting takes place and how long you think it might take. It is also worth remembering that the subject-matter of some meetings cannot be completed in a single session, and arrangements will have to be made to agree a timetable for a series of meetings.

(b) Organise a meeting place that is large enough and accessible to the participants.

(c) If travel is involved, ensure that your own travel arrangements are made (by you or someone on your behalf). As the junior member of a team, you might also be expected to organise, or at least coordinate, the arrangements for other members of your team.

(d)   If overnight stays are involved, ensure that suitable accommodation arrangements are made.

(e)   Confirm all arrangements with the participants (preferably in writing, with a copy to secretaries) so that they are all clear about them.

Before the meeting can actually take place, you must also be confident that any necessary domestic and refreshment arrangements have been made. In some firms, this will be handled by the firm's receptionists; in others, it may have to be your secretary.

As we shall see in 2.4, organisation also includes pre-meeting preparation by the people attending. Without it, much of the value of the meeting will be lost.

2.2.2   Purpose

All too often it happens that people who are invited to a meeting (or who expect to be there) waste their time. This is usually because they and the other participants are there for different purposes. Be clear in your own mind why the meeting is being held, and only invite people along who need to be there (rather than who want to be there); and before going to a meeting yourself, consider why you need to go. In the early days of your career, you may have little choice in whether you attend or not, but at least observe and learn from the experience of others.

For certain kinds of meetings, it may be appropriate to take along an expert of some kind (e.g., accountant, valuer, actuary, tax lawyer). If you decide to do this, although it may be tempting to 'spring' the expert on the other side, it is less than courteous to do that and may in fact be counter-productive if the other side adjourn the meeting in order to bring along their equivalent expert. If only as a matter of courtesy, therefore, inform other participants of the *dramatis personae* involved in the meeting.

2.2.3 Communication

No meeting can take place without communication. On one level, of course, this means that all the skills discussed in *Effective Communication* by Tony King (Blackstone Press, 1991) are relevant here. The expression of ideas in language that others understand, and the technique of active listening are vital.

However, on another level it also means not allowing a single meeting to develop into a series of smaller meetings simply because the participants hold their own conversations in groups of two or three. Whether this happens or not depends a great deal on the role of the chairman and the attitude (and manners) of those participating. Every step should therefore be taken to ensure that everyone present participates in the same meeting either by active communication or active listening.

2.2.4 Relevance

Another great time-waster is the tendency of participants to talk about things not relevant to the purpose of the meeting, or at least not relevant to everyone who is there. Being clear when you organise a meeting, or agree to attend one, why it is being held and what the participants intend to discuss is very important to keeping the meeting on course. Again, the role and authority of the chairman is very important. An agenda for the meeting will also help to keep people's minds focused on the relevant issues (see also 2.5).

2.2.5 Location

There is another issue that we can usefully consider at this stage, although it affects organisation. The question of where a meeting should be held excites different reactions. Some lawyers have distinct preferences about where they hold their meetings. You have five options:

(a) in your own offices;
(b) in your client's offices;
(c) in another lawyer's or adviser's offices;
(d) in another party's offices; or

(e)   on neutral ground (which might include property that is the subject of the meeting).

If a meeting is held in your own offices, it cuts down travel time, gives you control of the physical organisation and layout, may imply the right for someone from the firm to chair the meeting, and makes some people feel that they are in a stronger position and in greater control. All these things are true, but are not always as powerful as some would like to believe. Part of the problem with familiarity and the feeling of control is that you can miss some obvious or subtle things that are going on around you simply because you are feeling too comfortable.

Further considerations arise if you meet in your own offices. For example, you have to decide whether to meet in your own office or in a meeting room. Your own office may be less formal, but it will need to be tidy, large enough to accommodate the necessary number of people comfortably – and provide sufficient space for documents to be spread out and for notes to be taken – and not disrupt others around you (particularly if you share your office with another lawyer). Sometimes, simply walking other people through to your office can disturb others. The danger of breaches of client confidentiality is also a major consideration when outsiders are allowed to walk through working areas. The layout of the meeting space can also be used to create or remove physical barriers to effective communication. Finally, wherever you hold a meeting, do your utmost to ensure that you are not interrupted by unwanted telephone calls or visitors.

Meeting at someone else's office has some of the opposite features of those discussed above. The biggest advantage of these is not being too complacent about your surroundings and perhaps therefore being more aware of what is happening. On the other hand, if you want to stage a tactical withdrawal from a meeting for a short while, you may have the disadvantage of not knowing where to go to kick your heels. Being relieved of the responsibility for organising the meeting place can also be a great bonus!

Whatever you decide will have cost implications for your client: meeting in your own offices eliminates travel time and the direct cost of travel. Sometimes, neither you nor the client will have any choice.

For example, conferences with counsel are still held predominantly in counsel's chambers and counsel will 'chair' the meeting.

2.3 REASONS FOR HAVING MEETINGS

There are almost as many reasons for having meetings as there are meetings. In many cases, a meeting is held because someone, somewhere, thought it would be a good idea, though that is rarely a valid reason. The 'business' reasons include reaching agreement, settling a document, completion of a transaction, and pre-trial conferences. Whatever the variety of reasons, the underlying structure of all meetings is sufficiently similar for us to look at whether a meeting is the right method for the objective to be achieved.

If we regard meetings as a particular form or method of communication, we need to examine in what circumstances a meeting is a better form of communication than other methods (e.g., letter, telephone) given the objective or purpose to be achieved. For the most part, this will be because there is a reason for face-to-face contact.

Another factor in this debate is the advent of technology. The use of telephones, fax machines, voice messaging, and the electronic distribution of documents by computer all lead to a temptation not to meet people. The problem here is not so much that people meet when they do not need to, but that they do not meet when they should.

There are seven reasons why meetings become necessary rather than desirable. If a meeting is held for another reason, or lacks one of the essential elements described in 2.2, it is more likely to result in someone wasting time.

2.3.1 Volume

If there are many issues to be talked about or decided, or if the issues are going to develop and change as the discussions proceed, there is really no alternative to a meeting. Letters are inadequate for a large number of issues or an iterative process, and the telephone is often inadequate.

2.3.2 People

If there are several people who need to be involved in discussions or decision-making, having them all together is often the most effective way of reaching agreement. Letters are too cumbersome for 'discussion' involving more than a few people; and even though conference-calling is now possible by telephone, meetings usually result in better and swifter action, unless distance or economics dictate otherwise.

2.3.3 Complexity

In some discussions, the complexity of the issues involved is such that face-to-face contact is safer. There may not be many issues, and there may not be many people involved, but the outcome is too important to run the risk of someone not fully understanding what may have been written or said over the telephone. If you are explaining a difficult subject to someone, it is much easier to see whether they have understood if you can actually see their reactions, and be immediately available to follow up on furrowed brows or quizzical looks.

2.3.4 Deadlock

In many situations (particularly involving negotiating an agreement or settlement), only so much can be achieved without meeting – indeed, a meeting often becomes the only practical way of moving the parties towards a sensible conclusion. It is much easier for someone to be unreasonable when they are not actually facing you. Hiding behind the 'anonymity' of a letter or the telephone is the reason why many agreements are not reached, much to the disgust or disappointment of clients.

2.3.5 Urgency

Strange as it might at first sight appear, when time is of the essence, meeting the players involved can be much more effective than other forms of communication. The reason for this is that everyone comes together, they can all be sure about what they have agreed, who is going to do things, and by when.

2.3.6 Eye contact

When people or documents have to be examined or seen, there is obviously little effective alternative to a meeting. Sometimes it will be necessary to have site meetings, too. These are all instances of the need for eye-to-eye or eye-to-object contact.

2.3.7 Persuasion

One of the most difficult forms of communication is the art of persuasion. Whether you want to persuade a client to follow a course of action, or persuade another party or opponent to agree to your proposals, or persuade a prospective client that you are the right lawyer for the job, there is no substitute for doing it face-to-face.

2.4 PREPARATION

The success of any meeting increases in proportion to the amount of preparation you put in to it. It is true that for some meetings you will have little idea of how they will go and ultimately what issues you will need to deal with. But that is no excuse for not at least thinking about what might happen and being as well prepared as you can be. This does not mean preparing for every conceivable eventuality, though it does imply being as well briefed as you can be – about the client, the other parties, the other advisers, and the issues as they are known. It also means thinking through your own (or your client's) objectives. In the press of everyday client work, preparation is often the first casualty. This is not good for your clients, and in the long run is not good for your, or your firm's, reputation. Of course, in the early days, without the experience to know how meetings are likely to develop, preparation is much harder; and a lot will also depend on the extent to which you are both informed and involved by the lawyers running the matter.

Some part of preparation must be devoted by those running the matter to what they hope to achieve from the meeting, and what strategy or tactics they will adopt to do so. In order to do this, further information or investigation of options may be required (for which adequate time and resource should be set aside). Hopefully, these thoughts will be shared with you. At times it may also be necessary or sensible to have a 'pre-meeting meeting' with the client, to discuss information, objectives, options, tactics and attitudes.

2.5   THE CHAIRMAN OR HOST

The role and behaviour of the chairman or host can often determine the success, failure or achievement of a meeting. In most meetings, there will be no formal appointment of chairman. However, all meetings need someone who can guide them and keep the meeting and its participants on course. Without that guidance, the purpose of the meeting may not be achieved.

The question of who takes the chair or leads a meeting will usually be settled by common (and sometimes unspoken) consent. The choice may well depend on a number of factors, including who is acting as host, or who is the most senior lawyer, or who is perceived to be in the strongest position.

The role of the chairman or host is principally:

(a)   to make sure that the meeting is conducted in an orderly manner;

(b)   to be sure that all the issues that the participants are there to address are covered properly;

(c)   to see that those participants who have something to say have their opportunity and are listened to, but without dominating the proceedings;

(d)   at convenient points during the meeting to summarise the issues, discussions and decisions so that everyone is clear; and

(e)   to ensure that proper notes of the meeting are taken (and the chairman may want to appoint a note-taker before or at the beginning of the meeting if there is no formal secretary present).

If you know in advance that you are to chair or host a meeting, you should check that all arrangements have been properly made. You should also give some thought to the need for an agenda and its contents. If a formal agenda is not required (as will often be the case), the chairman or host should still think about the structure of the meeting and the order in which issues should be discussed, and may decide to produce at least a list of the topics to be discussed. Without some focus, there is a real danger that the meeting will go off at a tangent or that different participants will be working to their own, hidden, agendas.

There are many different styles of chairmanship. Again, if you go to a meeting, observe these differences and form your own views about what is likely to be the most natural way for you to conduct a meeting when your time comes.

If you have organised a meeting for a partner in your firm, be sure to tell him or her what arrangements you have made. Use your knowledge of that partner's style to determine or ask how you can give further help.

2.6 TAKING PART

In the early days of your career, 'taking part' in a meeting may be limited to just being there, carrying the files, hailing the taxi, or photocopying the agenda. If you are invited to attend a client meeting, seize the opportunity with relish: even if you are not more actively involved, make the most of the opportunity to learn from watching others and listening to them. A number of law firms do not encourage (and in some cases do not allow) trainee solicitors or junior assistants to attend client meetings. Given the chance, make the most of it.

As your career progresses, you will become involved in more and more meetings, and the level of your participation will increase. You may even be expected to 'take' a meeting at short notice when a partner or more senior lawyer is unexpectedly called away. This is when you will be (and will feel) at your most vulnerable. Your vulnerability will be reduced if you fully understand what the meeting is all about, what your client wants or needs to achieve from it, and you are as well prepared as you can be. Being nervous and inexperienced is no excuse for failing to do your best.

2.6.1   Giving your views

When you say something in a meeting, remember that quality is more important than quantity. Plan what you want to say, and say it as succinctly as possible. You will overwhelm participants if you go on too long, or give too many reasons why you think your view is right. Once you do that, they will switch off before you have finished – your best points may be lost in a haze of boredom or confusion. If you have a lot to say, break it down into smaller topics and make it clear to your listeners where you are in your own overall scheme. Pause regularly to give them a chance to ask questions, or to seek clarification, further detail or more explanation. Watch their faces and actions for signs of interest, concern, disagreement or wonder – these are all benefits you would not have by letter or over the telephone, so make the most of them.

When other participants are speaking, allow them to say what they want to without interruption. By all means at a suitable point ask for clarification of things you have not fully understood or would like further explained. However, if it is obvious that the speaker has more to say, let him or her finish before you make any substantive response. The motto here should be to behave towards others as you would want them to behave towards you. Very little can be gained in most meetings by being aggressive, rude or intolerant – whatever the provocation – and there is plenty of evidence that clients are not impressed by the sabre-rattling of obnoxious lawyers.

If the discussions falter over certain issues, do not feel that you must always press your point to a conclusion. Adjourning a meeting for further reflection or instructions is not necessarily a failure; forcing a conclusion may well prove to be. In some circumstances, a full adjournment may not be necessary if you can split up for a while for private talks with your client or with colleagues.

2.6.2   Things to avoid

It is impossible to give a complete guide on how to behave in meetings. The skills involved are a mixture of communication skills (dealt with in other books in this series) and normal social interaction, for which good manners will be your best guide. Nevertheless, there are some things that experience suggests are better avoided:

(a)   Do not lose your temper. Lawyers (and particularly litigators) will often take a perverse pride in trying to irritate their professional opponents. Do not rise to the bait. Such behaviour is unnecessary and immature; and however effective those lawyers will tell you their skills are, there is always another way to achieve the same result, consistent with decent behaviour and the strong representation of a client's interests. Such people are also themselves likely to become irritated when faced with someone who refuses to be drawn, and may decide to change their approach.

(b)   If you have a proposal to make, resist the temptation to make the proposal and then explain it. By the time you have finished your proposal (if not before), a lawyer's mind will already be thinking of the thousand reasons why your proposal cannot be accepted. Your reasons will be inconsequential, even though in fact they are crucial to reaching an agreement. Invert the process: explain your objectives and reasons for making the proposal, and then finish with the proposal itself. That way, you are not giving others much opportunity to do anything other than concentrate on what you are saying.

(c)   Avoid drafting in a meeting. Everyone knows that 'drafting in committee' is ineffective. Instead, agree who will be responsible for the draft, make notes of the points to be covered and the issues involved, and then let the drafting be done away from the meeting. If it is urgent, let the draftsman adjourn to another room. These suggestions hold good even if the purpose of the meeting itself is to consider a draft document, where amendments (other than the most straightforward) should also be drafted and incorporated after the meeting has finished.

2.6.3   Before you leave

All too often you will think during a meeting that you have understood what was discussed or decided, and who has agreed to do what, only to find when you return to your office that your recollection is not as clear as it should be. Therefore before you leave a meeting be sure that:

(a)   all the issues you wanted to discuss have been addressed: be clear about what was decided, and be equally clear about what you have not been able to resolve;

(b)   you have taken notes which will allow you to prepare a record of the meeting (see 2.7.1), and will enable you to take any necessary action or to follow up with those who should;

(c)   everyone knows what they have each agreed to do and the timescale involved.

Finally, given that it can be extremely difficult to organise times when everyone can meet, if another meeting is required it may be easier to organise it before they all leave than it will be when they have returned to their busy offices.

2.7   WHEN IT'S OVER

The end of a meeting is not the end of your responsibilities. As soon as a meeting is over, everyone's recollection of what happened and what now needs doing will begin to fade. Follow-up is a vital part of making the meeting successful.

2.7.1   Notes

One or more participants should have agreed at or before the meeting to produce minutes or notes of what happened. Because memories fade, these should be produced as soon as possible after the meeting.

The important elements of the note are:

(a)   factual: the date of the meeting, where it was held, who took part (and in what capacity they attended or acted), and its length;

(b)   content: a description of what was discussed, the decisions made, proposals accepted, and matters left unresolved;

(c)   action: who agreed to do what and by when; and

(d)   statement of author and date of the note.

Some authors of notes make the mistake of taking near-verbatim notes during the meeting itself and then reproducing them as a note of the meeting. This is not necessary, and is rarely even helpful. However, it is a good idea to keep on the appropriate file a copy of any handwritten or other notes taken during the meeting: if an issue arises in subsequent proceedings, this contemporaneous note could be used to refresh the author's memory when giving evidence of what happened at the meeting. If only for this reason, try to resist the temptation to doodle on your notepad during a meeting!

Certain types of notes of meetings will have to be agreed – particularly notes of a conference with counsel, which are often amended by hand, signed and returned to you. Copies of the minutes or note should be distributed to the participants (at least those on 'your side'). It may also be advisable to send copies to certain people who were not at the meeting to keep them informed of events.

2.7.2   Follow-up action

It is, of course, important that those who agreed to do something should actually do it, and do so by the time agreed. In 3.4 we shall look at various reminder systems. There is no excuse for forgetting to do something, so make sure that your own systems for reminding yourself work. It often makes sense to make notes of what other people have agreed to do (e.g., clients, partners or other lawyers with whom you are working, and even the other parties or advisers) so that you can remind or chase those others at the appropriate time.

2.8   SUMMARY OF KEY ISSUES

(a)   All meetings are potential time-wasters, but are more likely to be productive if they are called for the right reasons, are properly organised, have a defined purpose, encourage communication by everyone, and remain relevant to all participants.

(b)   The location of meetings is not an incidental issue, but may have a profound effect on the outcome.

(c)   The role of chairman or host is crucial to the effectiveness of a meeting, and should involve supervising arrangements for the meeting and its agenda (however informal), ensuring the smooth running of the proceedings, and the performance of any required follow-up.

(d)   The success of any meeting increases in proportion to the effort put in to preparing for it, and the constructive participation and follow-up of those involved in it.

Chapter Three

Moving Paper

3.1 INTRODUCTION

Lawyers are probably the most prodigious movers of paper of any profession or industry. Almost every aspect of their working life involves handling files, books, letters, memoranda, and so on. A look around the offices of many practitioners will convince you that professional negligence is an accident just waiting to happen. Do not believe that it will never happen to you – that kind of complacency is an invitation for a dissatisfied client at least and disciplinary action at worst.

Technology experts are talking about the 'paperless office', and a number of firms are already using electronic mail (E-mail) for internal communication. But even though technology has made great strides (and continues to do so), a law office that is literally paperless is still many years away. Until then, we must do what we can to control the organisation and flow of paper.

3.2 FILES AND FILING

The starting-point has to be an efficient filing system. There are very few law firms that do not have good filing systems – at least in theory. What lets them down is the way they are used. Take some time to understand the system in operation in your firm.

The most important files are client files: the efficient running of a matter demands that these files are properly organised and as up to date as possible. Many firms have more than one physical file for even straightforward matters – usually one for correspondence and another for documents and working papers. However, the complexity of the filing will depend on the complexity of the average matter. When more than one lawyer is involved on the same matter (particularly when a specialist elsewhere in the firm is involved), duplicate or 'sister' files are often created. When the same client uses the firm for more than one matter, related files will also exist. You can probably begin to see that the opportunities are legion for paper to go missing, for lawyers not to be fully informed, and for paper to be placed on the wrong file.

Everyone in the firm who handles a file has a responsibility not to abuse it. For instance, if you remove a document from a file to photocopy it, make sure you replace it, and that you put it back in the right place. Some firms file papers in chronological order, others in reverse chronological order: if papers are out of order, a lot of time can be wasted.

The key to efficient filing is the system and use of file numbering. In most firms, a file number is allocated as part of the file-opening procedure (usually handled by the accounts department or a records department). It is important that all documents and correspondence bear this unique reference. Many firms use a combination of client and matter number. This means that a client will have the same client number however many matters the firm handles for that client: again, the opportunities for misfiling are increased and great care must be taken to ensure that the correct matter number is used. On all correspondence you initiate, be sure to check that the correct file reference has been used.

For non-client files, the firm may have its own system which you should also adhere to wherever possible. However, you will always want to maintain some files of your own. Work out a filing system, and numbering or referencing method, with your secretary so that paper can be allocated to the right place and found again by both of you when required. (As a trainee solicitor, you may have to do all of these things – as well as the filing – yourself.)

In any office, the process of filing is regarded as a boring chore. It is nevertheless important, and though it might be boring it is not a mindless activity. Proper and efficient filing is the lifeblood (and often the life-saver) of a law office. At some point during your career, you are likely to have to do some filing: accept the responsibility with good grace and ponder the consequences of failing to do it properly. As you progress, emphasise to others how important it is and do not accept poor filing from anyone.

3.3 REVIEWING PAPER

Without a system for moving paper around your own office, your desk will quickly become a paper mountain hiding you from the rest of the world. Some lawyers delight in such a working environment – and often have an uncanny knack of being able to lay their hands on a particular piece of paper whenever they need it. For most of us, however, this is a recipe for inefficiency and frustration. Nor does it help when they are ill or away from the office and someone else needs to take some action.

The ideal principle is that, at any given time, you should only deal with a piece of paper once. This is not to say that you should only ever deal with each piece of paper once. What it means is that you should have a system that allows you to clear your desk of paper that you are not presently working on. To achieve this, you will need to divide the paper that crosses your desk into different categories, and then deal with each accordingly. Ultimately, there are relatively few options. Here are some suggestions.

3.3.1 Things to do

Some documents will require that you do something – reply, act, telephone, and so on. If this is the case, either act immediately or set aside some time in the future when you are going to do so (see chapter 5). If you act immediately, decide when you have finished whether you need to keep the piece of paper that prompted the action: if you do, file it; if not, throw it away. If you do not act immediately, either file the original or put it (or a copy) in a reminder system to remind you at the appropriate time that you need to take some action (see 3.4).

3.3.2   Incomplete action

Sometimes, you will be able to begin work on something but will not be able to complete it (because of lack of time or information, or because you are waiting for a reply, for example). Again, rather than leave the incomplete work on your desk waiting for your next attentions, put the paper in a reminder system (see 3.4) or, if it can – or should – be filed, file it and use the reminder system to bring a copy forward for review at the appropriate time. You can also put handwritten reminders into a system to prompt you to complete or resume action on a file.

3.3.3   Information

Law firms are often awash with internal memoranda and sundry other paper announcing developments that their lawyers should be aware of. (It is surprising how many internal notes are requests for missing files!) Too many busy lawyers simply put such notes straight into their waste bins and then complain bitterly that no one tells them anything.

Paper that is sent to you for information should be read as quickly as possible. It should then be filed if you need to keep it for future reference, or thrown away.

3.3.4   Circulation

Some paper (particularly journals) will be sent to you as part of a distribution list. The value of the circulated material will probably decline rapidly with time, so do not keep these items back. If you cannot read them within a day of receiving them, put yourself back at the bottom of the circulation list and send the paper to its next destination. Ask your secretary to do this sort of thing for you if you are away from the office on business or on holiday. You are of course at the mercy of readers further down the list (as, indeed, you are of readers above you), but if this proves to be a problem raise it with the firm's librarian (or whoever is responsible for organising the distribution list).

3.3.5 Reading material

Some people add a fifth category to cope with those pieces of paper or journals that they want to read during a planned 'reading time' (usually on a train or at home). Again, if journals are part of a circulation system, do not hold on to them for more than a day or two. Once read, the paper or journals should be filed, passed on, or thrown away.

3.4 REMINDER SYSTEMS

While it should not be necessary to remind lawyers about the importance of deadlines and time-limits, it is amazing to see how many firms have no firm-wide reminder systems, where lawyers are left to their own devices to meet deadlines as best they can. Those who are not inclined to record-keeping are often the ones you read about in the *Law Society's Gazette* in the disciplinary proceedings section. As professional indemnity premiums continue to rise, the insurers are paying closer attention to reminder systems. Since most claims are for missed deadlines and time-limits, particular care should be taken to establish and use these systems.

3.4.1 Reminders

A reminder (or 'tickler') system provides a written reminder of actions which must be taken within a specified time period. In litigation matters, this means that virtually every file must have an entry in the reminder system for some reason (e.g., limitation period, court hearings). This may be a pipedream, but if you were to approach your system from this standpoint and work at getting every file into the system, you would readily see the advantages. It is very unusual to find a firm where none of the lawyers must be prodded to do their work on time.

It is also very unusual to find a firm so fortunate that all lawyers are conscientious enough to keep their own tickler systems and to see that their work is done in a timely manner. There should be a firm-wide system, and lawyers should be required to use the system: this is a matter of quality control, and it must be regulated by the firm.

Someone must have the responsibility for maintaining a firm-wide reminder system if it is to be successful, and the librarian is usually given that responsibility. Firms too small to justify a librarian often give the responsibility to an office manager, legal executive or senior secretary. This does not mean, however, that the lawyers are absolved of all responsibility. Any reminder system is only as good as those who operate it. If your firm has such a system, make sure you understand it, use it and use it properly. In addition, of course, you should maintain your own diary with duplicate entries (which could be made by your secretary). This gives you a double reminder system (see 5.8.2 and 5.9.1) – the kind of cross-check that the indemnity insurers look on favourably.

3.4.2   Items to be entered

Any type of future commitment or action belongs in the reminder system. Examples would be:

(a)   All dates related to contentious matters, including: limitation dates; due dates or deadline dates for various pleadings; deadlines for notices of appeal; deposition dates; trial and hearing dates.

(b)   Follow-up dates for lease renewals, rent reviews, share options, annual reports, minutes of meetings etc.

(c)   Follow-up dates for review of inactive files or review of files labelled for destruction.

As a minimum, start this system with files that involve court dates, files that involve limitation dates, and matters in which there are time-limits.

3.4.3   How the system works

All firm-wide reminder systems are slightly different in their operation. This paragraph describes the principles on which many of them work.

To be sure that all necessary entries are made, lawyers usually complete a standard reminder form (which is often two-part or three-part carbonised) and submit it to the librarian. The reminder form will normally include at least such information as:

(a)   Client's name.

(b)   Client and matter number.

(c)   Name(s) of the matter partner and assigned lawyer(s).

(d)   Description of the matter (including if appropriate the name of the court and the action number).

(e)   Description of the action to be taken.

(f)   Deadline date (the date the 'time-limit' expires).

(g)   Action date (the date on which the work should be done in order not to miss the deadline date: this should be at least five working days before the deadline).

(h)   Reminder date (the date on which the submitting lawyer wishes to be reminded to take action: this should be at least five working days before the action date).

(i)   Name of submitting lawyer.

An example is included in appendix 1.

On receipt of a completed form, the librarian will put the whole form into the system, which will usually be organised chronologically. Initially, the form will be placed in the system in accordance with the reminder date. When the reminder date arrives, the librarian sends one part of the reminder form to the submitting lawyer and places the remaining two parts back in the system in accordance with the date by which action is required. When the necessary action has been taken by the lawyers, the form is crossed through, initialled, dated and returned to the librarian: the remaining form will then be removed from the system. If the first reminder has not been returned to the librarian by the time the action date arrives, the process is repeated with the second part of the form, though this time the librarian will also telephone the submitting lawyer and the matter partner. The librarian replaces the final part of the form in the system in accordance with the deadline date. If neither the first nor second part of the reminder form has been returned to the librarian by the deadline date, the submitting lawyer and the matter partner are contacted, and often the appropriate head of department as well.

Any reminder system is only as good as the people in the firm make it. Secretaries should also take some initiative in the process. Although you will have procedures that theoretically handle the system, dates will still be missed. Secretaries should be encouraged to watch out for dates that should be tickled. Lawyers write such dates on file folders, on notepads, on scraps of paper which may be put in a coat pocket and forgotten: the likelihood of a date noted in this manner getting into your system will increase if your secretary is trained to watch for them as well.

Not only must the secretaries be constantly alert for such dates but they should also assume the responsibility for seeing that the various forms for the system are completed and sent to the librarian.

Some computer systems now allow reminder systems of this nature to be executed electronically. As with any firm-wide system, it is a wise precaution not to rely on it entirely and to maintain a personal system as well.

3.4.4   Personal reminder systems

We have so far looked at firm-wide systems designed to save you from the calamity of missed court hearings, forgotten time-limits and the like. But there are many other events about which you will need reminding – to take some follow-up action, reply to a letter, talk to a client about progress, hold a review meeting with a colleague.

The archetypal personal reminder system is, of course, a diary. Some people use sophisticated time managers or filofaxes, and others use electronic diaries. Whatever the method, and whatever firm-wide systems there may be, there is no substitute for maintaining such a personal system.

The use of a diary is discussed in more detail in 5.8. The more organised lawyers will also have their own reminder, 'tickler' or 'bring-forward' systems. Such systems work in this way:

(a)   When a letter etc. is produced or received that you want to see again, a copy of it is marked to be seen again on a certain date. For example, if you need to take some further action, or if you write to someone and expect a reply, you can mark a copy of that letter to be seen again in 14 days' time. You can use this system to remind yourself of anything simply by making a note on a piece of paper to be brought forward at the appropriate time.

(b)   When your secretary receives these marked-forward copies, they are put into a folder organised chronologically.

(c)   At the beginning of each working day, your secretary takes out those letters etc. marked for your attention on that day and gives them to you.

(d)   If by then you have not received a reply, you can either write a reminder to the recipient or mark the letter forward again. If you have reminded yourself to do something, you can now do it.

(e)   When the reminder has served its purpose, the copy letter etc. can be thrown away.

This type of system is very easy to set up and use, and helps ensure that things do not get overlooked, and that not too much paper is allowed to build up (and get lost) on your desk.

3.5   PERSONAL KNOW-HOW

The practice of law is a process of providing know-how to clients – lawyers sell what they know how to do. In fact, the success and reputation of a law firm is based on the collective know-how of its lawyers and on its ability to transfer that know-how from lawyer to lawyer.

As a practising lawyer you will probably, over a period of time, collect useful precedents, letters of advice, articles and so on that you think you might want to refer to again. If you do this (and it is highly recommended), establish a filing system that will allow you to retrieve these useful items easily. For the most part, this will mean organising the paper according to its subject-matter or to the type of transaction to which it relates. Organising know-how materials by type of document or in chronological order tends to be popular but these are the least effective methods because they do not usually bring like materials together in the way in which you are likely to want to retrieve them.

A particularly useful form of personal know-how is a checklist. Such a list can relate to legal issues (e.g., circumstances in which *Mareva* injunctions will be granted), to procedural issues (e.g., steps in a takeover, flotation or a transfer of property), or to a specific matter (e.g., the things you must do to see the matter through to a successful conclusion). A number of lawyers dismiss checklists as unnecessary or even as an insult to their professional ability. It is satisfying to know that highly experienced airline pilots do not take the same narrow-minded view before they take an aeroplane off the ground.

An increasing number of law firms are now establishing firm-wide or departmental know-how systems to make their collected wisdom and specialist expertise more widely available. If your firm does this, make the most of these services since it can save you many hours of frustration and 'reinventing wheels' as well as improve your own performance, know-how and expertise.

3.6 SUMMARY OF KEY ISSUES

(a) Controlling the flow and organisation of paper is a very important task. Your firm's filing system must be understood and adhered to, and filing must be kept up to date.

(b) The timely movement of paper is vital to the efficiency of the office. Develop your own procedures for ensuring that you deal with paper as soon as possible, and keep the paper mountain off your desk.

(c) If your firm operates a reminder system, make sure that you understand it and use it. Create your own personal reminder system to bring forward items that you need to see and act on at certain times.

(d)   Develop your own know-how and collections of know-how materials. If your firm has departmental or firm-wide know-how or precedent systems, be an assiduous contributor and responsible user.

Chapter Four

Working with your Secretary

4.1 INTRODUCTION

Good secretaries are worth their weight in gold. Unfortunately, secretaries are only as good as you allow them to be, and too few lawyers really know how to work well with this invaluable resource. Too often, they make assumptions about what the secretary will or will not want to do or be able to do without even talking it through.

When you first arrive in a law firm, you are (understandably) anxious to prove yourself in a new, and often competitive, environment. Your head is brimming with the law you have learned, and you are desperate to put into practice the skills you think you have learned. Most secretaries have seen it all before – and are not impressed! Do not regard them as an intellectual punch-bag: they usually know more about the practice of law than you do at that stage (particularly in a small firm). Treat them as equals; in fact, treat them as specialists in what they do, and use that specialisation to help you. You need their support: few of them enjoy working with trainee solicitors because their written work is routinely changed (or even emasculated) by their principals and has to be done again. Your reputation will go before you, and you will have a much happier and productive professional life if you are recognised by the secretaries as a good person to work with.

To begin with, you will have to accept that you are unlikely to have your 'own' secretary – in fact, in some firms, trainee solicitors are not allocated a secretary at all, not even a shared one. The level of service and attention you receive will inevitably be less than the more experienced lawyers. You will have to live with this and make the best of the situation.

As you become more experienced and senior, you will come to expect a higher level of secretarial service. Much of that will still depend on the way you manage the relationship with your secretary, and many of the ground rules covered in this chapter remain valid.

Not all that many years ago, most lawyers were men – and so were their secretaries. This has changed, and the vast majority of secretaries now are women. In order to avoid cumbersome writing, this fact is reflected in the rest of this chapter – with apologies to male secretaries.

4.2 TEAMWORK

4.2.1 General observations

Start from the standpoint that neither you nor your secretary can do your jobs without the other. Your work will not be typed, your letters posted, your faxes sent, your appointments made and so on without her help. Similarly, your secretary's job does not exist in isolation. It should be immediately apparent that the key to success is teamwork between the two of you.

Sadly, you will hear some lawyers say how useless their secretaries are, how they never do even the obvious things, and cannot be trusted to do anything properly. On closer examination, you will find that very few secretaries are actually as bad as this (and if they are, they should not be staying). What these critical lawyers have is a self-fulfilling prophesy. Because they treat their secretaries badly and assume that they cannot do even the basics, their secretaries react badly to the way they are treated and certainly do not go out of their way to help. These lawyers would find that by spending a little time each day developing a working relationship with their secretaries their lives could be a lot more productive and their human relationships much more pleasant. Most secretaries are looking for challenge and stimulation in their working lives and welcome an opportunity to do something other than typing and filing.

In most law firms you are likely to find an 'us and them' attitude between the lawyers and the non-lawyers. There is fault on both sides, but the principal problem stems from the intellectual superiority claimed by the lawyers and their tendency to treat others as lesser mortals. It is true that client work drives a law firm: that is the business activity. But it does not follow from that that lawyers are the most important and intelligent people in a law firm – and even if they are, it is unbelievable arrogance to behave as such. This process starts with lawyers mistreating their secretaries, who often then take out their frustration on the firm's administrative staff. Without the cooperation and efforts of every member of the firm, clients will not receive a first-class service. Let us not waste time trying to demonstrate to each other how much better we are – save that for the market-place.

4.2.2   Shared secretaries

Law firms looking for more efficiency, particularly in the use of word processors and other technology, often require their fee-earners to share secretaries. If this is the case, of course, the opportunities for developing a close working relationship with a secretary are more limited. Nevertheless, if you again regard the secretary and the other lawyer as part of your team, you will begin to see ways of making all three of you more productive.

These situations are not always easy to handle. Suggestions for dealing with (or better still avoiding) conflicting pressures on a shared secretary are:

(a)   try 'negotiating' with the other, usually more senior, lawyer to achieve a result that satisfies everyone (including the secretary);

(b)   break up the work that you need doing into smaller elements so that your secretary can intersperse your work more easily with that of your colleague; or

(c) having broken up the work into smaller elements, you may be able to find another, less busy, secretary to help you.

Again, unfortunately, some lawyers will take delight in 'pulling rank' over a more junior lawyer and monopolising the use of a secretary. If you are the junior lawyer, you will find this phase of your working life difficult. However, do not match the professional selfishness and immaturity of other lawyers with responses in kind. Deal with these situations objectively and dispassionately. In any event, do not allow the secretary to become 'piggy in the middle' in a dispute between fee-earners about whose work is more important or urgent.

4.3 HELPING YOUR SECRETARY TO HELP YOU

The first piece of advice is to assume that your secretary knows more about your firm's office procedures than you do, and has more experience of working for lawyers than you can imagine. (Naturally, if you are allocated a new or inexperienced secretary this will not be the case.) So do not begin your relationship by laying down how you think things should be done, but instead discuss how things are or could be done and see if your new secretary has any ideas or preferences of her own. The principal areas for discussion follow.

4.3.1 Giving work to do

Find out when is the best time to give your secretary work to do. Most secretaries will prefer to have the work (or at least to be told about what is coming) as early in the day as possible. This will allow both of you to assess workloads, to establish priorities, and to plan the working day. This is particularly important if your secretary also works for someone else.

When you hand over dictation, some secretaries like a list of what you have dictated on tape, so that they can see what needs to be done. Others prefer to have the files to which the dictation relates, so that they can maintain a consistent layout and style, and check the spelling of certain names. Discuss these preferences or other possibilities, and establish a mutually productive working relationship. One particular reason for giving your secretary (or at least making for your own benefit) a list of what is on a tape is the possibility of a dictated tape breaking or being lost. The list will not prevent you from having to dictate the contents again but will at least give you a head start in knowing what was on the tape to begin with.

You may safely assume that your secretary will do your work in the order in which you hand it over, so if the priorities are different, be sure to make that clear.

For all these reasons, it makes sense to have a short daily meeting with your secretary to be sure you are both prepared for what you expect to happen (though always expect the unexpected to throw you out). Five minutes is often all it takes.

4.3.2   Diary maintenance

Discuss with your secretary whether either or both of you will maintain your diary. If you each keep a diary of your movements and activities, be sure you liaise regularly (at least daily) to be certain that they each mirror the other. Some lawyers will not allow their secretaries to make diary entries without their permission: this is acceptable, provided that, if you are not in the office, you are happy for your secretary to say to a client or someone else that she is not able to arrange or confirm a meeting. This does not always give the right impression. However, when your secretary does keep your diary for you, you must impress on her the important duty she has to remind you of meetings, deadlines and other things recorded in it.

4.3.3   Telephone messages

A secretary can provide a useful filter for telephone calls. You will probably find that most secretaries consider themselves too busy (or trainee solicitors too junior) for them to do this for you. You will have to reach whatever arrangement you can. However, there will always be occasions when you will not be in your office to take calls, and you should then be sure that your secretary will take messages for you. People differ widely in their ability to take messages, but if you are given a message you do not understand do not be afraid to ask for clarification – if you let people get away with giving you 'lazy' messages, that is the service you will always tend to receive.

A good message will tell you (legibly) who called, who the caller represents, the date and time of the call, what the caller's telephone number is, the substance of the call, and whether the caller will telephone again or you are expected to telephone him or her. (If you have to take a message for someone, remember these fundamentals.)

4.3.4 Preparation

If you are due to attend a meeting, your secretary may be willing to help you prepare for it by making sure that you have the necessary files, papers or materials that you need. Secretaries who take a real interest in their work (or, perhaps more correctly, in your work), may expect to do this. However, do not expect this service in the early days.

4.3.5 Travel arrangements

If you have to travel on business, your secretary should be prepared to make the necessary travel and accommodation arrangements for you. However, do not make that assumption the first time you travel. Establish with your secretary what you need and be sure that the arrangements will be made for you. Similarly, if you need a taxi for a local meeting, check with her beforehand that she will make a booking for you.

4.3.6 Filing and copying

One of the banes of any lawyer's life is the need to have a file up to date or to have documents copied. Depending on the culture of the firm you are in, secretaries may be expected to handle all of these things, or trainees may be expected to look after their own needs. If you are not sure, ask.

4.3.7 Routine correspondence

Check with your secretary whether it is necessary for you to dictate every letter, or whether for some routine or repetitive correspondence she will prepare a letter or draft on her own. Secretaries have different views about their abilities to do this for you, or about the extent of their responsibilities. A good secretary, however, will welcome the responsibility.

4.3.8   Reminder systems

We discussed the merits of firm-wide and personal reminder systems
in 3.4. Establish with your secretary whether she operates any such
systems and, if not, whether she would be willing to.

4.3.9   Domestic arrangements

Some secretaries regard it as part of their job to make tea or coffee,
and to organise sandwiches, for their bosses; others would be
positively resistant and hostile to what they see as an affront to their
professionalism. The same is true of their attitude to personal
correspondence, organising birthday and anniversary cards and
presents for spouses, or theatre and other personal entertainment
arrangements. Expect to do these things for yourself: if anything else
happens, regard it as a bonus!

4.4   DICTATING TECHNIQUES

A major part of a legal secretary's work is transcribing letters and
other documents dictated by lawyers. Few lawyers are trained in
dictating skills, with the consequence that many secretaries grumble
about the standard. A few brave ones take it on themselves to train
their bosses themselves!

For the most part, dictating effectively is a matter of common sense,
plus some cooperation between you and your secretary to establish a
system that you both feel comfortable with. The paragraphs that
follow, therefore, are mainly common sense.

4.4.1   Preparation

Do not approach your tape recorder with an open mouth. In other
words, do not even think about dictating until you have thought
about what you are going to say. If necessary, make notes of the
points you want to cover. In the early days, you may feel the need to
write out the whole of what you want to say so that you can simply
read into the recorder. This is acceptable as a short-term measure
while you get used to the idea of dictating, but it is a very inefficient
use of time (you talk about seven times faster than you write).

Make sure you have any details you need close to hand; copies of letters, files, addresses etc. should all be on your desk before you start. Once you begin, you will probably take undesirable short cuts so as not to interrupt your flow. Even if your best intentions are to check the details later, you will often find that you do not remember, or do not have the time, or your secretary sends the document out on your behalf because you were not in your office in time to get it in the post.

Almost everyone is embarrassed when they first start dictating – more so if they have to share an office with a more experienced lawyer. We have all been through it, so try not to think about it: the odds are that the other lawyer has much better things to do than listen to your first faltering steps sitting in the corner of the same room 'talking to yourself'.

4.4.2 Identify yourself

Until your voice becomes well-known to your secretary, it might be a good idea to give your name at the beginning of a tape. There are other good reasons for this:

(a) In a busy office, the tapes of a trainee solicitor or junior assistant are not always transcribed by his or her regular secretary. If tapes are distributed, the secretary who actually transcribes the tape needs to know who she is listening to.

(b) At some time during your career, a tape will go missing (usually with the results of several hours' deliberation and carefully chosen words on it).

In some offices, the tapes themselves are marked in some way to identify the author – for example, initials, colour-coded stickers: this serves exactly the same purpose.

4.4.3 Urgency

If there is a deadline by which the tape needs to be completed, say so; you should also confirm this to your secretary when you hand over the tape. Again, it may not be your own secretary who transcribes the tape, so you are making sure that whoever does it knows the urgency.

In fact, the best advice is always to dictate urgent letters or documents on separate tapes, so that they can be more easily distributed to other secretaries to make sure the time-scale is met. If an urgent letter is hidden away amongst other less urgent documents on a tape, it is much harder for secretaries to meet your deadlines.

In the same vein, dictate your letters on tape in the order of priority for having them returned to you. The whole tape may not be transcribed on the same day, so at least you will have the more important or time-sensitive documents returned to you first.

Finally, there are some lawyers whose work is always identified by them as urgent. No-one has work that is in fact always urgent. If they think it is, it means either that they have been so disorganised or inefficient in arranging their workload that things are always left to the last possible moment, or that they are selfish in the way they use the secretarial resource. Do not be one of these people. In your own eyes, you may appear to be more important if your work is always up against a deadline; but in the eyes of others you may be seen as bordering on the professionally incompetent.

4.4.4   Enclosures

Most authors think about the enclosures they need to go with a document when the document has been finalised and is ready to go. However, if you need enclosures to be printed off or copied, or worse still prepared, your secretary will not thank you (and is in danger of missing your deadlines) if you leave them as an afterthought. Better still, then, to indicate to your secretary at the outset that the document she is about to type will need certain enclosures. If need be, she can then start organising their production or copying while the document itself is being prepared, so that the document and its enclosures are ready at more or less the same time.

This applies to other, less obvious, forms of enclosures like bankers' drafts and cheques. Every firm will have a requisition procedure to go through. There is more chance that a cheque will be ready to go with your letter if you or your secretary set the procedure in motion sooner rather than later.

4.4.5 Type of document

During the course of your professional life, you will dictate many different types of documents: letters, memoranda, faxes, agreements, instructions to counsel, statements of claim, and so on. Depending on your firm, it may have different types of preprinted paper (for example, letterheads, faxes, internal memoranda). If your secretary still uses a typewriter, she will need to know what sort of paper to put in her machine before she starts: you know and she does not, so be sure to tell her what type of document you are dictating. Even if (as most now do) she is using a word processor, different types of documents are set up using different 'formats' for document layout, and she will still need to know what sort of paper to load into the printer (or which printer or print tray to use).

You will often want to reflect on or review a letter or document that has been typed for you, and many times you will want to change it. If so, it is an expensive waste to have it printed on the firm's letterhead or on engrossment paper. In all cases, indicate on the tape that your intention is to produce either a draft or final version of the document.

4.4.6 Instructions

Many letters that you dictate will carry certain warnings or instructions which the secretary will record at the head of the letter. Common warnings are: Subject to Contract, Subject to Lease, Without Prejudice, Personal and Confidential. A particularly frequent error is to mark a letter 'Confidential' or 'Personal', but not the envelope. This rather defeats the purpose, so be sure to check both before the letter is sent.

Instructions usually relate to the method of delivery and could be: By Fax and Post, By Hand, By Courier, Air Mail, Recorded or Registered Delivery, and so on. These instructions also need to be repeated on the envelope so that when posting time comes the secretary remembers or the mail room know what is appropriate.

4.4.7 Order

Reference was made in 4.4.5 to the different layouts or formats of documents. You will notice from copies of these various documents that certain types of information always appear in the same place and in the same order. For instance, most letters will require a name and address, followed by your reference number and then the recipient's reference number. An internal memorandum will require details of sender, recipient, subject-matter, and reference number. Look carefully at the various forms or layout used in your own firm, and consider from the secretary's point of view the order in which she will have to type the contents. You can then do her an enormous favour by dictating the information to her in the right order. Until this order is second nature to you, keep a selection of the firm's preprinted stationery to hand so that you can refer to it as you dictate. Bear in mind, however, that some secretaries will consider it part of their job to look up and type in addresses and references: establish what your secretary prefers before you run the risk of irritating her by dictating things she does not expect to hear.

4.4.8   Dictating style

This is an area where people will differ, and secretaries will react in different ways. Be aware that there is more than one way of doing things, and find ways that are helpful to both of you. The following points are fairly standard areas of potential difficulty:

(a)   Spell names, words that are unusual or difficult, legal words or expressions and other jargon, and so on. However, be guided by your secretary: if she has the file, she may prefer to check spellings for herself, and she may have wide legal experience and so understands all the technical expressions already. Talking to her to find out what she prefers, and trial and error to establish exactly what she can and cannot do without assistance, are the keys here. If you do spell names or words on tape, remember that people in some walks of life use a phonetic alphabet to make their spellings clearer. One is included in appendix 2 which you might want to memorise and use.

(b)   Be very careful when dictating numbers, whether they are part of a sum of money, a date, or something else. To someone who is listening, there is little difference in sound between '£19,000' and '£90,000' – but there is a lot of difference to the person paying or receiving!

(c) Your firm may have its own conventions dealing with the layout of documents (though it would be unusual if it did: this is usually left to the preference of the individual lawyer or secretary). Over a period of time, you and your secretary will get used to each other, so that for the most part layout will be dealt with by short and simple expressions: for example, 'Stop' indicates the end of a sentence marked by a full stop; and 'New para' indicates the end of one paragraph and the beginning of another. However, modern laser printers can give you a wide range of attractive features in the layout and presentation of your documents, producing bold and italic print in the same document, columns, and so on. You will have to work out with your secretary how to give clear instructions on these points.

Sometimes you will want to include a quotation in a document. Most people set these within quotation marks in a separate paragraph indented from the rest of the document. One way of indicating this would be: 'New para, quote indented, open quotes . . . close quotes, new para'.

The use of headings and numbering systems can be a source of particular difficulty. However, see if you can imagine what the following document would look like – what follows is what a secretary would hear (using commas to indicate pauses to you): 'New line, main heading, bold caps, B THE FACTS, new line, subheading bold, one point one Background, new line, We act for Acme Power Plant, open brackets, open quotes, caps APP, close quotes, close brackets, stop, The relevant facts are as follows, colon, new line, indented, in brackets, lower Roman one, APP was the subject of an article in the, italics, Blackacre Morning Post, end italics, of fourth March nineteen ninety stop, new line, indented, in brackets, lower Roman two', and so on. Hopefully, what the secretary will produce is:

B.   THE FACTS

1.1   Background

We act for Acme Power Plant ('APP'). The relevant facts are as follows:

(i) APP was the subject of an article in the *Blackacre Morning Post* of 4th March 1990.

(ii) . . .

One particular nightmare is dictating a long document and losing track of your numbering system for headings and paragraphs. One way to overcome this is to keep a separate note of the headings you have used or where you have reached in the numbering system (this can also be useful for cross-referencing to other parts or paragraphs of the document). Better still to keep to a consistent system, so that secretaries do not become confused by different styles, and can help fill in the odd gap or correct the odd slip for you.

Secretaries also differ in their approach and attitude towards the dictation of punctuation. However, there are many lawyers who cannot punctuate properly, and at the end of the day a document must go out as you want it. If your secretary is better at punctuation than you are, let her do it for you (and take steps to learn yourself); if you have any doubts, dictate the punctuation you want.

4.4.9 At the end

When you reach the end of a document, say 'End of letter' or something similar: your secretary will then know that she has reached a convenient break. Before you start the next item, explain whether you will need copies of your document to go to other people: if so, say how many copies you will need and who they should go to. If you want everyone to know who has had copies, you can add a distribution (or 'c.c.' – originally 'carbon copy') list to the document: these are known as open copies. Sometimes, however, you will want someone to have a copy of the document without the addressee knowing: this is known as a blind copy. Be sure to give your secretary the appropriate instructions.

If your document is to be posted, you should also think about the packaging arrangements. For letters, your secretary will assume (rightly) that an ordinary envelope is required. However, your closer knowledge of what will actually be sent to the recipient may mean that you appreciate that, with enclosures, a different size or strength of envelope is required. Again, be sure to tell the secretary so that she does not waste time and envelopes preparing something that will not be required.

When you reach the end of all your dictation on a tape, say 'That's all on this tape': your secretary will then know that she does not need to keep listening to the tape just in case there is something else on it that does not begin immediately because you left the tape running before you started again.

When work is returned to you for checking, make sure you check things very carefully. The eye is very good at seeing what your brain remembers saying, but that might not be what is actually written. Check the following particularly carefully:

(a) a missing 'not' that can completely change the meaning of your message;

(b) 'than' or 'that', 'what' or 'that', 'their' or 'there', and so on, in place of each other;

(c) the spelling of names, and the accuracy of addresses;

(d) that names, addresses, and mailing instructions are properly repeated (on both the letter and the envelope);

(e) that pages are correctly numbered and ordered, and that enclosures are present and in the most logical order (usually the order they are referred to in the document); and

(f) that the envelope used is both large enough and strong enough to take all the papers and to withstand the rigours of the postal system to its destination.

4.5 DICTATING MACHINES

Now a few words about the dictating machine itself and how it affects the way you dictate:

(a) Regard the recorder as you would any other microphone. The quality of the recording will be adversely affected if you hold it too close, or too far away; or if you stare at the floor, the ceiling or out of the window; or if you eat, chew gum or smoke while you are talking.

(b)   Many microphones are particularly sensitive to ambient noise. If you are looking for something, moving papers around, or sharing a room with another lawyer who has a lot of people dropping by or who spends a lot of time on the telephone, that background noise might also be picked up and make it more difficult for your secretary to hear what you are saying.

(c)   The recorder will not instantaneously start recording when you switch it on: allow a second or two before you start speaking so that the first crucial words or syllables are not missed. The same is also true when you stop speaking, so do not cut yourself off by being 'trigger-happy'.

(d)   Very few people can dictate without pausing. You will often want to stop to consider your next sentence or paragraph; you will all too often be interrupted by the telephone and other distractions. When this happens, be sure to switch the recorder off while you pause, think, or are interrupted. If you do not, the secretary will have to sit there listening to silence, background noise, or other conversations. In a similar vein, try not to stop and start too much, because the 'noise' of the recorder being switched on and off is caught on tape, and if it happens too much can be very irritating to the secretary.

(e)   Following on from point (d), bear in mind that your secretary will probably be operating her transcribing machine with a foot pedal. If you can maintain a steady, even pace in your dictation, you will help her to maintain a steady, even pace in transcription. In this context, you should also be aware that if you are reading from something, you will speak rather more quickly than you would normally: so if, for instance, you incorporate a quotation from another document or a law report, make a deliberate effort to slow down a little.

(f)   Although you might feel as though you are sitting in your office talking to yourself, do not forget that you will be listened to by someone who would prefer to be interested in what she is typing. Imagine, therefore, that you are talking face to face, and put some energy and expression into your voice. In this way, not only will you be more likely to keep your secretary's interest, you will also be more likely to make yourself more readily understood.

(g) Most recorders have a light on them to show that the machine is recording. Keep an eye on this light: many authors have discovered that they have sat talking only to themselves for several minutes!

One final thought – and one reflecting a situation over which you may have little influence – is that if your only dictating machine is a large, desk-top system, the only place you can dictate is at your desk. This will not always be convenient (because of emergencies, interruptions and so on). Consider using a hand-held, portable machine either as your standard equipment or as a fall-back that you can borrow on those occasions when you need to dictate away from your desk.

4.6 SUMMARY OF KEY ISSUES

(a) Your relationship with your secretary will be one of the most crucial of your office relationships: begin on the right footing by being professional in your dealings with her and expect the same in return. The keys to a good working team between you and your secretary are discussion and mutual respect.

(b) Sharing secretaries is becoming more common and requires other skills of forethought and diplomacy.

(c) Discuss the best ways of handing work over, maintaining your diary, taking messages, helping you prepare for meetings, dealing with routine correspondence, filing and reminder systems.

(d) Before you dictate anything, prepare yourself by collecting the information you need and the thoughts you want to express. Bear in mind the urgency of the work you are dictating, its type, and enclosures you may need.

(e)   Develop a dictating style that is clear and helpful, and use your dictating machine intelligently.

Chapter Five

Managing Yourself and Your Practice

5.1 INTRODUCTION

Lawyers tend to lead busy and reactive lives, often feeling that their time is controlled by others. They show a fascination in the techniques of time management in the mistaken belief that some simple and easy-to-apply solutions exist that will allow them to exert control for themselves and so become more productive.

The truth is that in no walk of life is there such a thing as time management. You simply cannot manage time: it is inflexible, perishable, and once gone cannot be replaced. You cannot make it or keep it. It is a precious resource that you can use or abuse. What we are really talking about is personal management or self-management to make the best use of time.

The objective of most lawyers is (or should be) to work 'normal' hours. What is normal varies from firm to firm, and depends on the nature of its practice and its culture. Obviously, some late and weekend working is required of all professionals from time to time in order to cope with client crises or unexpected developments. If, having taken all reasonable steps to achieve this objective, late or weekend working becomes part of the normal pattern, pressure or stress is likely to result and the quality of your performance will (whatever you believe) inevitably decline. The problems of dealing with pressure are discussed in chapter 6.

5.2   RECOGNISING THE PROBLEMS

You have to recognise and accept that you will never be in complete control of your professional life, and it is futile to try. Nevertheless, it is possible to exercise more control and coordination than most lawyers do.

Lawyers tend to bill their 'chargeable' time to clients, and in order to maximise profit they need to charge as much of their time as possible (there is more to say about this subject in 5.10, including whether lawyers should in fact charge for time at all). When they look at the number of hours they have available, and how many of them are actually chargeable, most lawyers are disappointed. Time has obviously been spent on other things, and if it was not chargeable they often think it must have been wasted.

This attitude pervades the profession and leads it to avoid or downgrade many important activities that are essential to the smooth running and success of any business. Being client-driven (or, in your case, more likely, being partner-driven) is not an excuse for being badly organised. Certain things just have to be done, and personal management requires that you force those things into the time you have available. It is certain that you will not be able to expand time to accommodate all the things you would like to do.

Ask any group of lawyers what stops them getting things done or wastes their time and you will receive a variety of responses. Chief among them will be:

   (a)   The telephone – it interrupts, you can never get hold of the people you need to speak to, messages are not returned, and so on.

   (b)   Administration – it requires that you fill in forms for everything, and bombards you with bureaucracy and paper (incidentally, good administration does neither of these things, but such is the average lawyer's disdain for the administration in his or her own firm that these notions are hard to shift).

   (c)   Meetings which do not achieve anything – we discussed this in chapter 2.

(d)   Not knowing what the procedures are, where to find things, who to talk to – this is often the result of inexperience as a practitioner, or being new to a firm, and will improve with time.

(e)   Slow decision-making in the firm – usually the result of inadequate or inexperienced management.

(f)   Socialising – talking to people in the office who drop in or meet you in the corridor as you fetch your coffee.

(g)   Daydreaming (from the honest ones!).

(h)   Clients (from the cynical, naive or cavalier ones). More often than not, what lawyers see as client nuisance or interference is a sincere desire on the part of the client to find out what is going on because the lawyer has not bothered to keep the client informed. If more active steps were taken to do this, clients would have far less cause to telephone their lawyers at inconvenient moments.

In all these instances, lawyers can do something to control the effect of these 'time-wasting' events. What they illustrate is the highly reactive nature of a practitioner's day, and basic unwillingness to do something positive if it involves even a short while doing some planning.

5.3   YOUR IMMEDIATE ENVIRONMENT

The first step in self-organisation is to control your immediate environment, starting in your own office and particularly your desk. If your desk, and the floor space around you, is covered in paper, you cannot work efficiently. Even if it is all arranged in neat piles, you are falling at the first fence. Make good use of filing cabinets (and filing systems) to move paper off your desk. Use the principles discussed in chapter 3 to keep the paper moving. Keep books and journals in a bookcase. Leave room on your desk to work freely on whatever needs to occupy your current attention, unhindered by what you were doing yesterday, or by what you must remember to do tomorrow. Keep a notepad and pens and pencils handy for when the telephone rings; have your secretary prepare a list of telephone numbers you regularly use. If you must have paper on your desk, use filing trays to distinguish one pile of paper from another, and allow your secretary to help you keep a tidy desk (assuming she is willing to help you in the first place).

5.4   TAKING CONTROL

With even a small amount of effort and organisation, lawyers would begin to reap the rewards of the 80-20 principle – that, in broad terms, 80 per cent of productivity comes from 20 per cent of time. It may not be possible to control all of your time, but it certainly does make sense to try to control the 20 per cent that produces the most or the best work.

The first step is to control the things that you know will happen. Principally, this will be for one of two reasons:

(a)   Something is going to happen whether you want it to or not, and whether it is convenient or not – for instance, a court hearing or other form of meeting, or events that are regular, routine or recurrent. You can begin to organise your time around such events, planning the preparation and follow-up time you will need.

(b)   You can make something happen when it is more convenient for you – for instance, making a call or arranging a meeting. Again, you can begin to exercise control around these events too. However, this does not mean excluding or ignoring the convenience of others – particularly clients. Organising for your own convenience does not mean being selfish and, indeed, selfish actions will lose you more clients than you keep.

Beyond this, recognise other opportunities for control. Persuade your secretary and others not to disturb you when your door is closed or at certain times of the day. Some people reserve mornings for meetings and afternoons for 'open house' interruptions. This does not mean making yourself completely unavailable, but educating those around you over a period of time. Some lawyers insist that they must always be available and open to interruptions: this may be true for some, but should still not become a licence to abuse your time. Recognise in the early days that you will have far less scope for control, but do not let that stop you thinking about how you could make things different so that when you have the chance you do not simply continue letting others 'steal' your time.

5.5 QUALITY TIME

The sole objective of personal management is not simply to make more time available or to make time more productive. Rather, it is important to improve the quality of available time so that you can work better and more productively – as some people put it, to work smarter, not harder.

Being human, we are all different. Some people work much better in the mornings, and others later in the day. Most people do, however, experience a dip in attention in the period after lunch. Learn to recognise these times in yourself. You will work much better at your own peak times, and as far as possible you should try to organise the more mundane and routine tasks for the times when you are naturally less alert.

By and large, we all want to get things done quickly, particularly those things that we do not relish. One tip for these tasks is to try to do them when everyone is not also trying to do them. For example, if you have to travel somewhere, it is much slower and less pleasant during the rush hour: if you can travel earlier or later (or even the night before, if you are going some distance and can afford to stay somewhere overnight), do so. Similarly, if you want to buy sandwiches, or draw money out of a bank, doing it at lunch-time will take you many times longer than at 11.30.

5.6 PRIORITIES

All lawyers have difficulties with priorities, not because they do not have them but because they are constantly changing. Few of us are fortunate enough to have only one task to do at any given time, and so the problem of assessing renewed priorities is an everyday activity. For most people, however, the choice is just as likely to be made on the basis of the seniority of the person who gave them the job to do, or who shouts loudest or longest, or who has the meanest reputation.

As a trainee solicitor or junior assistant, your priorities are very likely to be determined for you, though without consistency and often even without thought of the consequences on other aspects of your time or work. You will have to learn to deal with these conflicts as best you can, though staying silent, grinning and bearing the consequences is not always in clients', the firm's or your own best interests. You will be in a much better position to deal with the situation if you have a clear and objective idea of your workload. Let us examine how to assess priorities (even if you do not stick to them).

5.6.1 Things to do

Before you can assess what your priorities should be, you must know what you are responsible for doing, therefore create and maintain on a daily basis a personal things-to-do list. Not everything falls into the same category. For example, some of the things will be major projects that will take some time, or will be part of long-term matters you are handling. Other tasks will be to write letters, make telephone calls, organise meetings, and so on. Do not therefore keep a single list, but divide it into different activities you must undertake. If you use a proprietary filofax or time manager, it may be designed to help you in this process.

5.6.2 Timescale

For each task, you must also have some idea of when it must be completed. Without this, you may be tempted to deal with the easy or short tasks first, leaving insufficient time to handle those which require preparation, thinking or substantial execution, or the involvement of others who may not fit into your timescale.

It is also a good idea to estimate how long you think it will take you to complete each task, taking into account the things you must personally do as well as the response times and activities of others who are involved. You may have to undertake some preparation, research, drafting, follow-up and so on. When you first try to estimate, you will be stabbing in the dark; but do not let that deter you – it is only by having a guess and seeing how far out you were, and why, that you will ever become more accurate. This may become crucial later in your career when clients ask you how long things are going to take: 'Well, it all depends on . . .' is not a satisfactory answer.

5.6.3 Establishing priorities

Once you know what you have to do, you can assess the priorities of those tasks, and the relative priority of new tasks.

There are only two factors which should enter your assessment: urgency and importance. Do not confuse the two. Urgency relates to the time within which the task must be performed, and usually implies a deadline. Initially, the deadline may be some way off, but as time goes by the task becomes more urgent. Importance can be a harder assessment, because it is usually much more subjective. The task may be important to a client, to the firm, to a partner within the firm, to you personally in terms of your personal or career development, or to the world at large. Be as objective and impartial as you can.

Remember that something that has to be done immediately may be trivial, but it is still urgent. Another task can be very important to you, but does not have to be done for several days, and so is not urgent.

The result is that you can assess the relative priorities of the things you have to do, in decreasing order of importance, as follows:

(a)   the urgent and important;

(b)   the urgent but not important;

(c)   the important but not urgent; and

(d)   the neither urgent nor important (tasks that have remained in this category for some time ought to be delegated to someone else).

It probably does not make sense to try to categorise all the things you have to do in this way. But it will help you determine what you should be doing next. You will have to maintain some sense of tasks lower down the list so that you can assess whether you will in fact have time to attend to them before it is too late.

5.6.4   The special problems of long or difficult tasks

For all lawyers some of the time, and for others most of the time, long or difficult tasks will dominate their working life – a major trial, a planning enquiry, a takeover bid or defence, and so on. Forcing yourself to 'manage' this type of work can present a significant challenge. Looking at the whole job, and even persuading yourself where and how to start it, can be daunting. The key in all cases is to break the job down into more manageable units, setting your own targets for the conduct and completion of each part, and using your own personal systems (diary, reminders etc.) to ensure that the project progresses smoothly. You may need to build in a certain amount of flexibility or 'insurance' time to cope with delays or unforeseen difficulties.

You may also need to ensure that these all-consuming cases do not interfere with your other workload. Here, you may need to delegate all or part of your other work to other lawyers in the office. You should also consider dividing your time in the office so that part of every day (or week, or whatever is appropriate) is earmarked for activities that do not then become neglected by pressure of other work. Such time is as important as anything else you have to do and should be regarded with equivalent commitment.

5.7   PLANNING AHEAD

As we have seen, it is very difficult to plan very far ahead. However, based on the things to do list, you will know that you have certain tasks to complete within a certain time, and you anticipate that they will take you so long to do. You should also have some sense of your priorities. You then have some basis for planning time in your diary to carry out these tasks. Remember that you will hardly ever be able to sit down and just do one thing at a time, so make sure that the 'elapsed time' you allow is greater than the estimated time for carrying out the task. For example, if you have a job that must be finished in five weeks' time, and you think it will take you a week to complete, it is not wise to pencil in a start date four weeks away.

These suggestions should not be read as implying that you should schedule your work in endless detail and with military precision – you would spend too much time planning and not enough time doing. However, if you do not control what you must do and keep a very close eye on when it must be done by at least making some effort to plan the time to do those things, you are in danger of failing a client, your principal, and, above all, yourself.

If you have this sense of your responsibilities and priorities, you are also much better placed to talk to others about your workload and your ability to take on new work. This is not to suggest that you should indicate to senior partners that you are overloaded, but that you have an objective basis for discussing what you can handle and, if you do have too much, to have it reallocated before it is too late. Never take the risk with clients' affairs that you might be able to create more time out of thin air to do the things you must. If in doubt, talk to your principal, head of department or the relevant client partner.

5.8 USING YOUR DIARY

If you regard a diary as something in which you enter appointments and birthdays, you will probably use it simply as a reminder of meetings you have arranged. At least you should not then miss any appointments or suffer the embarrassment of having agreed to be in two places at the same time. However, you will be in danger of underusing a valuable tool. Of course, some people now regularly use proprietary time managers or filofaxes, or even computerised diaries, which allow them to carry out many more personal management functions. But with application, it is possible to use the traditional diary to cover many of the things that these more sophisticated (and more expensive) offerings allow.

You will need to agree with your secretary what control you will allow her to exercise over your diary, ranging from complete control to organise your life for you, to no control, providing her with little scope to help others when you are out of the office (see 4.3.2). Of course, as a trainee solicitor or junior assistant, you may have some difficulty in finding a secretary who is even prepared to be interested in your whereabouts and commitments.

5.8.1   Appointments

It is naturally important that you use your diary to make a note of meetings, whether external or internal. The message here, however, is not just to make a note of the time of the meeting. Estimate how long the meeting will take; earmark time to prepare for the meeting and to follow up after it; and if the meeting is away from the office, allow time to travel there and back.

If you carry your diary about with you, you might also note the address and telephone number of external meeting places. In this way, you will not forget where you are going once you are in the taxi, train or aeroplane, and will be able to telephone ahead if for some reason you are delayed.

5.8.2   Deadlines and reminders

We discussed reminder systems in 3.4. Your diary can also be a private reminder system. Make a note of any deadlines you need to be aware of: limitation dates, court hearings, option or lease expiry dates, and other important time-limits. Do not confine your entries to the expiry dates, but also build in some warning dates so that you have time to carry out any necessary action or research. Equally, do not use your diary as a substitute for a firm-wide or departmental reminder system: use it as an additional safeguard.

There will be other things that you might want to be reminded of: to write a letter or make a telephone call; to follow up on something that you would have expected to have heard about; to prepare certain pleadings, and so on. All of these things can be recorded in your diary, but again in addition to any other reminder system that you might operate (like a 'bring-forward' system). You need to be satisfied that if you are unexpectedly away from the office, you do not cause unnecessary difficulties for others – particularly clients who might suffer from some consequences of inaction or oversight.

5.8.3 Undertakings

Undertakings given by solicitors are regarded with great seriousness. An undertaking must always be fulfilled, whatever the cost to the solicitor concerned, and whether he has been put in funds by his client or not. It is regarded as a personal obligation of the solicitor who gave it, and should therefore be given only when the solicitor concerned is sure that he or she can comply with it. Breach of an undertaking is regarded as a serious disciplinary matter. For this reason, many firms forbid their trainee solicitors from giving undertakings.

Such serious obligations must not be overlooked, and the diary is one obvious place in which to record undertakings given and received. In due course, you will want to record those given by you personally, but make it a habit to record any undertaking given by any lawyer involved in a matter with you and do not hesitate to remind them at the appropriate time that they need to do something. As with other reminders, give yourself a warning period within which to carry out any necessary action before the undertaking deadline expires. Similarly, record undertakings given to you (or your firm or your client) so that you can check that the required action has been undertaken.

5.8.4 Long-term reminders

Most diaries only allow you to record reminders for a little beyond the calendar year to which they relate. Some of the items that you want to remind yourself about may well take you beyond the life of your diary. In this case, use the 'Notes' or a similar section of the diary to record these long-term items together. When you have a new diary, you can transfer these items to the appropriate date or to a new long-term section. As before, these entries ought to be duplicated in a firm-wide or other reminder system operated within the firm.

These long-term lists also serve another purpose. If you leave the department you have been working in (which is very likely for trainee solicitors) or leave the firm altogether, you have in one place a list of the important dates that whoever takes over your files needs to be reminded about. The process of preparing hand-over or leaving notes becomes much easier and more valuable if you can do this rather than having to root through several files to extract the necessary information.

5.9   MANAGING YOUR DAY

A belief that no form of control can be exercised over a lawyer's working day leads many to assume that only meetings can be planned, and the rest is reactivity. The cynical view is that control means planning down to the minute what to do and when to do it – which we all know will not work, so planning must be a waste of time. This, like so many views of management, is simplistic and naïve. Let us look at the different activities you may undertake during the course of a working day.

5.9.1   Reminders

We must start with the things you have reminded yourself to do today. Your diary or a reminder system will have brought something to your attention. Depending on what it is, you may be able to deal with it swiftly, or it may need more time. Whichever it is, you have reminded yourself for good reason, and so you must schedule some time to deal with the task: this may be as simple as slotting an extra job in with other things you must do during the day, or it may require you to set aside more time as a separate activity (see 5.9.4). Remember, however, that missed deadlines and undertakings are the most frequent cause of complaint and action against solicitors.

5.9.2   Meetings

The one thing that most people will schedule time for is meetings. But even here, what they often do not allow enough time for is preparation, travel and follow-up. All are predictable, so schedule some time for them. We will all be late for a meeting from time to time, but for some practitioners it is a way of life. Such behaviour is discourteous and unnecessary – far from giving the assumed picture of a busy professional much in demand, most people see it as a sign of being rude, disorganised and inefficient.

5.9.3   Letters and other documents

Every day you will have incoming and outgoing post to attend to, as well as other documents to read or prepare.

If you are operating a reminder system (see 3.4.4), have your secretary bring to you each morning copies of all the letters and memoranda you sent out the previous day. Review their contents, and consider when you would like them brought to your attention again: this will allow you to reflect with a fresh mind on what you did the day before, and if necessary take appropriate steps to limit the damage likely to be caused by hasty comments, overreaction or mistakes you missed.

As soon as the day's post is brought to you, make time to look through it – in fact, plan time early in each day to do that. As you read through it, divide it into different categories: items that can be filed, those that need a short response, and those that need a considered response. The filing can be sent for filing. If you can manage it, dictate your short responses there and then; otherwise, put them on one side to be dealt with later in the day. Those items that need a considered response should be marked forward to a time when you can give them due consideration: if that is likely to be today or tomorrow, by all means put them to one side, but if not have them brought forward by your reminder system.

Most days produce some routine or unchallenging correspondence. It is a good idea to get this out of the way quickly. This will move unnecessary and unwanted paper off your desk, and give your secretary something to be getting on with early in the day. In fact, as discussed in 4.3.7, you may want to train or allow your secretary to handle some of this correspondence for you.

The point with all of these things is that you know that you will have to do them, so develop a working habit that gets them done quickly and early. This does not mean being so formal as to enter time in your diary (though by all means do that if otherwise you or your secretary book your time so tightly that there is little space for these tasks). It is a question of giving yourself time in whatever 'game plan' you have for the day.

5.9.4   Deliberation time

The previous paragraph dealt with those letters and memoranda that require little intellectual effort on your part to produce. There will of course be more substantive documents – letters of advice, draft agreements, instructions to counsel, and the like – that will require prolonged thought and preparation. Similarly, you will need time to prepare for meetings and to think about tactics for some of the matters you are handling. You may also need to conduct research and prepare research notes.

All of these things require time, and as much of it without interruption as you can manage. Whenever you can, plan the time to do these things. You may achieve the freedom you need by closing your office door, going to the firm's library (or even a local one), or working from home (though for many of us, that means outside normal working hours). In your early professional days, you will have to accept that you will have less control over your ability to achieve these things.

5.9.5   Telephone

Many lawyers regard the telephone as the bane of their lives. It always rings at the most inconvenient times, or when you are not quite prepared to talk to the caller.

Some lawyers, and firms, take the view that they always have to be available to talk to clients and will therefore take every call that comes in. This is not necessarily good practice. The effective handling of one client's affairs will often require that you give them undivided attention without interruption from other clients (who will also expect your undivided attention when it is their turn). After all, if you are in court or out at a meeting (and how many use that as an excuse for not taking calls!), you will not always be available. A good secretary should be able to filter the calls that really are worth interrupting you for.

Of course, if you are not available to take incoming calls, you must be confident that effective messages are being taken (see 4.3.3). Once you have finished your period of solitary confinement, you must be sure to return the calls that came in for you. In this way, callers will realise that they can in fact leave messages for you that are passed on and to which you respond. This will give them confidence in the future to do the same thing and accept that you do have periods of unavailability which do not have catastrophic effects on your handling of their affairs.

As far as outgoing calls are concerned, you already have much more control simply because you can choose when to initiate them. Some calls you will not be able to postpone, and in order to carry on with your own work you will have to make them. Others, however, are not so critical, and your use of time will be far more effective if you group a number of calls together – preferably in the afternoon, when inland telephone rates are cheaper. As with all things, you should group the calls in order of priority. You might also experiment with fixing a period of time within which you expect the calls to be completed: this will improve your assessment of the value of the time you spend on the telephone, though hopefully without encouraging you to be brusque.

Preparation is also as important for telephone calls as it is for other aspects of your practice. Make sure that you have pens and notepaper to hand, together with any necessary files, papers, books etc. that you might need during the call. Even for incoming calls, think quickly what you might need; if necessary, ask for time to find them before the caller reaches full flight and before you have to interrupt the flow to lay your hands on a document he or she is referring to. Similarly, if you initiate the call, give the person you have called time to do the same.

Some telephone calls will be so important to you or to your client that you might consider rehearsing your opening words – they can be crucial to the subsequent tone and outcome of the conversation and will repay practice.

Never attempt to continue a telephone call if there is any indication that it is not convenient to the other person. You must have their full attention for the call to be productive, so do not blunder on if you feel that the attention is not there – even if your call is likely to be very short.

One of the principal problems of the telephone is the 'ping-pong' that people play trying to reach each other. If you do not immediately get through, do not 'hold the line' waiting for the other person to become free. Talk to the secretary and either establish when it will be convenient for you to call back, or give a time range during which you will be available to take a return call. This will not always work, of course, but it is preferable to the endless to-ing and fro-ing that might otherwise ensue.

Finally, one particular problem of modern technology is the hands-free 'speakerphone' which broadcasts telephone conversations more widely than one of the parties may intend. In the right circumstances, conference calls can be invaluable and provide an excellent way for several people to communicate with each other at the same time without meeting together. However, when used for two-person calls, they can become irritating. In fact, client surveys show that at least half of all clients object to talking to lawyers who use the speakerphone rather than picking up the handset. The reasons they give are potential lack of privacy, poor voice quality and echo, that it feels impersonal or patronising, and a feeling that the lawyer's complete attention might not be with the client. A conversation that others might overhear will put clients off. If you have a speakerphone, the best advice is to follow proper telephone etiquette and ask the caller's permission before using it.

5.9.6 Notes

We have already referred to the need to plan time for following up on meetings, and the desirability of planning some time to allow you to do that. Notes of meetings and attendance notes of telephone conversations are part of the process of the ordinary working day. They take time to produce, and their value declines with the length of time that elapses between the event and dictating the note. Be sure to allow time to produce them. Ideally, you should not leave the office before dictating your attendance notes for that day.

5.9.7 Interruptions

Even the best-planned days suffer from interruptions. We tend to regard all of them as bad, but in learning how to deal with them, we have to start by accepting that this is not the case. You will always have interruptions, and some of them are a necessary part of your work. You must learn to recognise the good ones from the wasteful ones. With the latter, there are three things you can do:

(a)   Do not work in such a way that you encourage others to interrupt you: examples are working with your office door always open, and always being willing to stop working to talk to someone who telephones you or walks into your office. This is not to suggest that you should therefore always work with your door closed, but being aware that there are times when you need to be closeted and that you may be working in such a way that you are making yourself open to interruptions.

(b)   When you estimate how long something is going to take you, use your experience of the likely level of interruptions to increase your estimate of the time involved. In this way, when you have been interrupted you will not feel under so much pressure to make up for 'lost' time.

(c)   Behave towards others in your office with due consideration for the value of their time. If law firms were able to develop this mutual sense of value, much less time would be wasted. Indeed, in some offices, internal meetings and calls are discouraged during certain hours of the day so that everyone knows that they will have some time free from internal actions disrupting their productivity (most lawyers, though, believe this is both impossible and undesirable).

A delicate problem is how to encourage someone to leave when you have other things to do. There are no magic solutions. Possibilities are to remain standing (or to stand up), find a reason to leave your office (to fetch a drink or answer a call of nature), or invent a meeting to go to or a train to catch. Best of all, however, would be working relationships that allow you to say that you have work to do and could you catch up with each other later.

A particular problem arises for those of you who share offices with another lawyer. You will be constantly interrupted by telephone calls and visits to your companion and the dictation that he or she does (and vice versa, of course). This is perhaps the worst of all types of interruptions. Achieving peace and quiet for yourself is virtually impossible. Between you, you might be able to establish a joint working arrangement that leaves both of you free at certain times to concentrate quietly, or to take calls and receive visitors. There are no easy answers, and you may be faced with the prospect of trying to find somewhere else in the office (an empty meeting room, or the library) where you can work relatively undisturbed.

5.9.8   Timesheets

Few firms these days do not require the keeping of timesheets (see further 5.10). Even if they only have to be submitted weekly, you will soon learn that if you do not complete them on a daily basis you will quickly forget what you did all day even yesterday let alone a week ago. Make the completion of timesheets part of your daily routine. Inaccurate information about time may lead the firm to draw many wrong conclusions about its performance and profitability: play your part in submitting accurate and timely information.

5.9.9   Daily review

Before you leave the office, it is a good idea to check that you have attended to all the things that needed doing today, and consider (however briefly) the things that will claim your attention tomorrow. In an idle moment, you can think about tomorrow and be just that little bit better prepared for it.

5.10   TIME RECORDING

For many lawyers, time recording is a burden – a type of 'spy in the cab' mechanism that they would prefer to do without. In order to understand the proper role of time recording, and your own role in its effective use, we must look at the development and wider benefits of time recording.

5.10.1   Advent

Time recording was first 'sold' to the legal profession as a way of measuring the cost of providing legal services. By comparing the hours spent on various aspects of client work with the overhead cost of running the practice, the hourly cost rate (or expense of time) can be calculated. For many lawyers, these calculations were a revelation. They had no idea how much it actually cost them to serve clients (except by referring to the total cost of overheads); they had only a 'feeling' that their charges were rendering a profit; and they consistently underestimated the time they spent on client work. Time recording was, then, a major contributor to greater financial awareness within many law firms and for some of them resulted in increased billings.

5.10.2 Hijack

Unfortunately, however, time recording was then hijacked. From knowing the hourly cost of providing legal services, it is but a short step to adding on a profit element and coming out with an hourly charge-out rate – a charge that can be used for calculating fees based on the amount of time spent on a client's matter. On the face of it, this is a fair way of charging clients for legal services (at least compared with the old method of weighing the file, counting the letters, and guessing at what the client could afford). But subsequent experience has shown that the ability to record time shows nothing more than the ability to record time. If clients are charged by the hour, there is little incentive for lawyers to carry out their work quickly and efficiently, for the longer they work on a matter the more a client will have to pay.

Such a system has no intrinsic merit. It overlooks the value of a matter (and of the advice given), and bears no necessary relation to the expertise brought to bear by the lawyer involved. We all know that a piece of advice that may save the client many hundreds or thousands of pounds can be given in a very short space of time; conversely, relatively simple advice may take longer to produce and have less value to the client. So we have been hooked on a system designed for one purpose being used for a different purpose for which it was not designed and is ill-equipped. Time-based billing rewards the inefficient and even the incompetent, and may not reward the truly high-value advice. Of course, lawyers have tried to overcome this unfairness by adding on a further profit element (permitted by the Law Society's professional rules) when the value of the transaction or advice reflects complexity, speed, value or various other factors. Clients do not particularly object to this, but they are never too happy to receive low-value advice for which the lawyer insists on a minimum time-based fee.

This confusion of time with billing has resulted in many unfortunate side-effects. The performance of lawyers, or even whole departments, has been assessed on their ability to record time and turn that time into fees billed. Whole appraisal and reward or bonus schemes have been built around the fallacy of the results of time recording. Promotion, career development and even redundancy have been decided on the mirage of these figures.

Client surveys show that clients distinguish between effort and results when they assess whether they receive value for money from their lawyers, and their principal (or only) focus is on results. Time-recording at best can only measure a lawyer's effort: it bears no relation to the results perceived by clients. It is therefore a very crude approximation to assessing the value of legal services to clients.

5.10.3   Real purpose

The only real value and purpose of time recording is to provide management information on the basis of which partners can make sensible and informed decisions about their firm. The information can be used for billing purposes, but only to determine the real cost of providing advice: the challenge being offered by clients now is to find a method of billing that reflects the value of the advice given and which is fair to both lawyer and client (rather than just to the lawyer).

The information that the firm can glean from its time recording system includes the following:

(a)   The way in which time is spent by various lawyers or departments: this will typically include both chargeable and non-chargeable time. From this information, the firm can determine the average time spent on chargeable work, how long certain matters usually take to handle, where there are peaks and troughs within departments and between departments, how much time to budget in the forthcoming year for various levels of lawyer in the firm (or even for specific lawyers), how much time is spent on research, training, marketing, management, and so on.

(b)   On the basis of recorded hours, the firm can create budgets and cash-flow projections, and establish financial standards against which to monitor work-in-progress levels, financial performance and profitability.

(c)   Variations in workload can be used to establish staffing and recruitment needs.

These are all vital management activities which, without time recording, would be difficult and in some cases impossible. The partners do not in fact need a time-recording system to allow them to assess fees (although it may provide useful additional information), and they should not need it to know whether their lawyers are working hard or hard enough.

The popular misconceptions about the role of time recording continue to lead many lawyers astray. They also result in the imaginative and creative recording of time: lawyers whose performance will be measured against targets based on time recorded will do all they can to ensure that they meet their target. This may mean over-recording time on certain matters, keeping work to themselves that they should hand over to someone more senior, more junior, or more specialised, and generally stacking the numbers in their own favour. Once this happens, the value of the information recorded becomes negligible – even for the purpose of assessing individual performance.

5.10.4   Your role in time recording

The purpose, therefore, of you recording how you spend your time is simply to record how you spend your time. This must be done as accurately as possible if the information is to have any value. Above all, therefore, you must remember not to make performance or billing decisions at the time you fill in your timesheet. Faithfully record the time you have actually spent on your various activities. It is someone else's decision to decide how much of your time is to be billed to a client.

There are some grey areas where different firms have different policies or, indeed, no policies at all. Take the following situations:

(a) You are asked to research a particular point on behalf of client A. It takes you five hours. The next day, someone else asks you to prepare a memorandum on exactly the same point for client B. It takes you one hour. Do you record five hours, one hour or three hours for each client? The answer is to record the actual time spent: the billing partner is the person who decides how much the advice or memorandum is worth to the client. Even if the point you researched is something that you felt you should have known anyway, you should still record how you actually spent your time. You may, of course, want to put a note on the relevant client file to remind the billing partner of the issue when he or she reviews it for billing purposes.

(b) During the course of a matter, you spend several hours with a more senior lawyer not producing anything of value to the client but in being trained or supervised. It is clear that the client should not be charged for this time, so establish with your supervisor how the time should be recorded – as chargeable time that will be written off, or as non-chargeable training time.

(c) As you become more senior, you will realise that there are other grey areas. For example, the time that you spend supervising other lawyers involved in a matter; the time you spend as a specialist answering detailed questions on points of law or practice arising from matters being handled by other lawyers in the firm; the time you spend being 'entertained' by clients looking for some free or cheap advice from you. In each case, the principle should remain: record accurately the time you actually spend on each activity. If it relates to client work, whether your own matter or someone else's, record the time against that matter: the appropriate billing partner will make the charging decision at some subsequent time. Your subjective judgments about the value of your time to the client are not your judgments to make.

Be sure that you understand whatever time-recording policies your firm has, and if you are ever in doubt do not hesitate to ask – you will probably find that some experienced lawyers are just as unsure as you are!

5.11 SUMMARY OF KEY ISSUES

(a) Time is a precious commodity and you must organise yourself to take best advantage of it.

(b) Organise your own office for maximum efficiency and keep your desk as tidy as you can, using filing cabinets to house paper you do not immediately require.

(c) Control those things that you can by planning around the events that you cannot organise yourself, and by organising other events for times that are convenient to you.

(d) Determine your own quality time and make best use of it for work that requires maximum attention or intellectual capacity.

(e) Develop things-to-do lists, assess priorities on the basis of urgency, importance and time-scale, and schedule time to deal with them.

(f) Use your diary as a sophisticated tool for recording appointments, deadlines, reminders, and undertakings.

(g) Plan each working day to deal with those things that must be accomplished (reminder actions, meetings, dictating, thinking, telephone calls, follow-up notes or records, and timesheets).

(h) Understand the proper role and importance of time recording, and play your part in its efficient operation in your firm.

Chapter Six

The Problems of Pressure

6.1 INTRODUCTION

Most lawyers work longer than 'normal' hours. Usually they enjoy what they do and want to put in the 'extra' time. This is all part of the professional lifestyle, and does not mean that all lawyers are workaholics. At some time during your career, you will feel distinctly under pressure. It cannot be avoided. The pressing and conflicting needs of clients will result in irreconcilable priorities that even the best organised and most skilled people cannot avoid. These difficulties become dangerous in people who do not recognise them or who, having recognised them, and refuse to do anything about them.

Working hard, and often during 'unsocial hours', is part of a lawyer's lot – particularly a commercial lawyer. Most will recognise that persistently working beyond normal hours is not good for one's professional or personal life, but that doing so occasionally is necessary. In some firms, the culture requires lawyers to be seen at their desks whether they have things to do or not, and even during evenings and weekends. Such is the path to partnership. Whatever we might say about the inherent stupidity of such action and culture, each of you must make a choice. If the culture in your firm, and the pressure of peer-group views, requires such antisocial and unproductive behaviour of its lawyers, you must make the decision whether you want to remain at the firm in the hope of becoming a partner. The decision is yours to make.

Some readers will find it difficult to identify with the theme or contents of this chapter, or with the suggestions in it. Perhaps they never will. But those who have experienced the problems of pressure will see only too clearly the merits of what is suggested, so do not dismiss too lightly the 'skills' put forward here.

6.2 SOURCES OF PRESSURE

Let us start by examining the different ways in which pressure can arise.

6.2.1 Professional pressure

The archetypal professional pressure is the feeling that there is too much work to do and not enough time in which to do it. This pressure may emerge from the client or from within the firm. The result is that you tend to work longer hours, take work home with you in the evenings and at weekends, and worry constantly about what you need to do.

At certain times, this pressure will be universal – there will simply be more work than your firm or department can comfortably handle. There is little point in making a great show about being overworked, unless the pressure or workload is not evenly distributed. You will have to do your best, but certainly not up to the point where your health suffers or the quality of your work declines. This will always be difficult: too much work to handle will almost inevitably result in unsatisfactory delays in getting through your work, and in a decline in quality, which ultimately can only lead to dissatisfied clients and perhaps disciplinary action. You will not initially be in a position to influence work acceptance by the firm. But rest assured that there is no merit in continuing to accept work where there is no reasonable prospect that it can be handled competently and within a reasonable timescale. Lawyers will always be judged on the quality of their work and service: once those begin to decline, the market-place will pick it up very quickly and the flow of new work will soon slow down or stop. Short-term gain can very soon become long-term disaster. Question whether such a firm is the right place for you to stay.

The key to handling any workflow is to be as well organised as you can be. That is what this book is all about. If you manage yourself well, you will soon know that you are going into overload. Armed with your own sense of organisation, you will find it much easier to persuade others, not by the subjective assertion that 'I'm too busy', but from an objective assessment of your workload and its implications for your time and performance.

When you do become busy, do not fall into the trap of doing the easy or short tasks first. Remember your priorities (see 5.6), and plan to use your time effectively. Very few matters are so desperate or crises so imminent that you have to drop everything to see to them immediately. Try not to become reactive when the pressure is on because that is when you start to lose what little control you have.

One particular pressure for trainee solicitors and junior assistants is the feeling that there is just too much to learn. Learning is, of course, all part of the process of professional development, but there will be times when this feeling is overwhelming. Often, you might feel that the answer to a problem that has eluded you for several days must be so obvious that you would look stupid to ask anyone to help. If you really have missed the solution for that long, the odds are that it is not that obvious. Take the risk, and ask someone who you think will be sympathetic. Most lawyers remember going through these difficulties and only the arrogant with no sense of professional responsibility would decline to help. For the most part, they would rather help you get it right than have to sort out a mess later.

This is not to imply that you should go running for help as soon as you have a problem – no-one will respect you for that. But talking through a problem, even with another trainee or junior assistant, will often help you see the real issues and begin to grope towards a solution.

Another sort of pressure in a busy office will arise if you do not feel you are busy enough. Provided your work is of sufficient quality for partners and senior lawyers to want to give you more work, do not hesitate to go and ask for more.

Finally, if you feel under pressure to do something that you consider to be illegal, dishonest, improper or unethical, do not do it, whatever the pressure.

6.2.2   Environmental pressure

This is, in fact, very similar to professional pressure. We are all affected by the human environment in which we work. Sometimes this manifests itself as the firm's 'culture'; sometimes it is the result of the way in which people in the firm treat each other. For example, some lawyers exhibit a 'macho' culture that does not allow them to admit that they do not know something or that they need help – they work all hours, and are generally disdainful of anything that is not earning fees. Other, more sensitive, people can find this a highly pressured environment. If this is coupled with internal politics, or an office where people do not respect each other's views or time, the result can be devastating.

For younger, or more junior, staff these types of environment can be thoroughly demotivating and very stressful. One of the greatest feelings of pressure we all experience is the feeling that we are not able to exercise any control over our immediate environment. As a more junior member of the team, you will of course have to accept that you will have little say in what sort of work you do, or how you do it, or who you work with. This is again all part of the process of learning your craft. But be clear what it is you do not like. If it is simply being a junior member of staff, you will just have to bide your time; if it is the wider environment in which you work, you may be able to do something to change it – if only, in the last resort, by going somewhere else.

6.2.3   Health problems

If your health is not what it should be, your work will suffer. Most firms are sympathetic to medical problems, and will allow you time to recover.

6.2.4   Domestic problems

A death in the family, divorce, or other marital or family difficulties will also usually draw sympathy. It is difficult to keep your mind on clients' affairs when emotional difficulties in your own life are close to the fore. What counts equally, though, is your attitude to coping with these personal problems. If you bring them unnecessarily into

the office, or for too long a period, without apparently trying to solve
the underlying issues, expect the sympathy and understanding to be
short-lived.

6.3 SYMPTOMS

It is one thing to be able to recognise the causes of pressure in our
lives, it is quite another to be able to recognise the symptoms of that
pressure that would prompt us to begin looking for the causes. Listen
to your close friends, since they are often the ones to ask first whether
there is anything wrong. If you are irritated by their enquiries and
concern, there probably is something wrong – or at least you are
perceived to be acting as if there were.

The symptoms are many and varied; some are dramatic (blackouts
and palpitations), others less so (headaches). But remember that they
are all danger signs of varying degrees. If you ignore the early
warnings, you may be afflicted by more serious problems later.
Self-preservation is not a sign of weakness.

The symptoms may be:

   (a)   repeated or persistent headaches;

   (b)   irritability;

   (c)   loss of motivation or interest in your work;

   (d)   loss of confidence in your ability;

   (e)   feeling tired all the time; broken sleep (especially waking up
with a work-related problem on your mind);

   (f)   loss of appetite; nausea or indigestion;

   (g)   turning to 'comforts' (e.g., more cigarettes, food, drink,
sleeping pills or other drugs).

Not all symptoms are physical. At times, you may feel that you have lost your confidence or self-esteem. You lose the will to get up in the mornings and go into the office. You lose your motivation, or feel more inclined to take time off for minor ailments. Many people will experience these feelings at some time. Recognise them for what they are – signs of pressure (or, at the other extreme, boredom) and time for a change.

6.4   MOVING FORWARD AGAIN

The solutions to alleviating these symptoms, as well as the underlying cause of the pressure itself, will be as many and varied as the symptoms and causes. The first step, however, must always be a recognition that there is a problem, combined with a willingness to do something about it. The solution may be a mixture of talking to someone within the firm, medical help, counselling, and taking steps to regain control. Normally, the person you should talk to and the nature of any medical help or counselling required will be self-evident. Regaining control is usually more problematic and, to be sure, somewhat more philosophical, involving as it does restoring a sense of proportion.

6.4.1   Doing something

The first step in regaining control is to start doing something. This means:

(a)   Control what can be controlled – this was the message in 5.4, and adopting the precepts in this book will help you in the management of your professional responsibilities.

(b)   Accept what cannot be changed. Not everything will go your way, and you can never influence every aspect of your life. Do not waste time and energy wishing things were otherwise unless you really can change them.

(c)   Review your priorities. Make sure you have them in the right order (see 5.6), and that you are truly spending your energy on things that need doing now.

(d)   Do not feel you have to respond immediately. Part of the process of exercising control is not being reactive. There will inevitably be times when you must respond at once, but these situations are not as common as many would have you believe. Provided you respond professionally, you need not respond immediately.

6.4.2   Communicate

The solution to many problems will become apparent simply by talking them through with someone who is prepared to listen. Sometimes, it is not even necessary that the listener fully understands what you are saying, just that they listen. Better of course if you can talk to someone within the firm who has a sympathetic ear, particularly if your problem is pressure for professional or environmental reasons. But, as they say, 'A problem shared is a problem halved'.

6.4.3   Deal with today

You cannot change history, and tomorrow is another day. You can expend considerable energy worrying about what might happen if.... On occasions, you will need contingency plans to help you cope with foreseeable, or even some unexpected, turns of events, but do not carry that to extremes. Also remember that what seems like an insuperable difficulty or impending disaster today can disappear after a night's sleep or the simple passage of time. Try not to create problems where they might not exist. Organise yourself for a productive day today (see 5.9), and derive satisfaction from using that time properly.

6.4.4   Think positive

Trite, but true. Problems become a lot more bearable if you can find a positive side to them. Feeling that the whole world is against you is not only unproductive and unhelpful, but also untrue.

6.4.5   Look after your health

All pressures are easier to deal with if you are fit. Find out what suits you, and exercise or take up a hobby that gives you fresh air and mobility. It need not be violent exercise – a regular, brisk walk will often do the trick. Spend some time out of the office each day (even if you only go to fetch your own sandwiches!). Eat and drink sensibly, and try to take as much sleep as you know you need. Do not sacrifice your holiday time, and if you have been working hard take at least a long weekend before things really get on top of you.

6.5 CONCLUSION

Standards in the legal profession are high and often uncompromising. However much it might be in the firm's interests to get the work done and keep the clients happy, it is also in its interests to make sure that it obtains the best from you.

If the pressure is still regularly too great for you, you will have to review whether you are in the right firm or even in the right profession. You owe it to the firm, to its clients, to the profession, but above all to yourself to be honest in your answer.

6.6 SUMMARY OF KEY ISSUES

(a) Learn to identify sources of pressure, whether connected to work or your working environment, or arising from outside your professional life. Determine whether these sources are temporary or permanent, firm-wide or departmental, universal or personal.

(b) Learn also to identify the physical, emotional and social symptoms of pressure, both in yourself and in others.

(c) Consider the best way of responding to the specific source and symptoms of pressure that you are experiencing: do what you can, share the difficulties, and work positively towards improving your lifestyle and approach to work.

(d) Keep a sense of perspective.

(e) Ultimately, review your career objectives and consider whether you might be happier, healthier and more productive in another firm or in a different walk of life.

Chapter Seven

Personal Development

7.1 INTRODUCTION

However much formal training you are given by your firm, and however great your exposure to new opportunities and challenges, you will never have all the skills and knowledge you need. In this chapter, we look at ways in which you can help and assess yourself as you move towards that elusive goal of partnership.

7.2 SELF-TRAINING

Whatever stage you have reached in your career, never overlook opportunities to learn more or to develop new skills. The advent of compulsory continuing education has focused lawyers' minds as never before on the need for continuing training. Not all of it is relevant, and much of it is wasted in the pursuit of the necessary number of points rather than the pursuit of knowledge or improved performance. Nevertheless, there are opportunities out there, so be sure to make the most of them.

A number of the professional skills you will need are covered by other books in this series. In addition, technology awareness and training, and wider management skills are becoming more important. Practising law is not just about knowing the relevant law and practice, but about operating efficiently in a business environment.

7.3 SELF-APPRAISAL AND PERSONAL DEVELOPMENT

7.3.1 The idea

Over recent years, a number of law firms have adopted the habits of the wider commercial world. One of those habits is appraisal. The systems differ markedly, and not all of them offer the opportunity for self-appraisal. However, in all walks of life (though perhaps more particularly in professional life) self-appraisal is important and should be encouraged.

The role of a practising lawyer is now recognised to involve a wide range of knowledge, skills and qualities. It is easy to resist the invitation to define them because we all know an elephant (or in this case a good lawyer) when we see one. But do we? Objectively, there cannot be a definitive list of qualities and requirements, but we can at least attempt a description. Periodically, assess yourself against the list that follows. Do it critically and with an open mind. If you have doubts, ask your principal or supervisor at an appropriate time (during an appraisal, for instance). You will find that the relevance and importance of some of the criteria will change over a period of time, reflecting your own development as a practising lawyer and your increasing involvement and responsibility.

7.3.2 The criteria

I *Subjective criteria*

A *Technical competence*

1 *Legal knowledge*
  Demonstrate a broad range of legal knowledge, with some expertise in your areas of practice and strong aptitudes for increasing your expertise in given areas of law.

2 *Research ability*
  Be capable of efficiently and effectively performing both legal as well as factual research and applying it to the situation at hand.

3   *Written work*
     Demonstrate expertise in the law as well as the ability to
     communicate clearly and effectively.

4   *Oral presentation*
     Demonstrate an ability to communicate clearly and effective-
     ly, whether to groups or to individuals.

5   *Organisation*
     Be organised in your workplace and in your daily routine.
     Timeliness and the ability to manage unusual situations
     effectively and professionally is very important.

B   *Professional competence*

1   *Conduct*
     Act responsibly and fairly, exercise good judgment, and be
     dependable in keeping up with the expectations of clients, the
     firm and the profession.

2   *Goals*
     Set goals for your professional development, monitor your
     progress towards them, and obtain assistance as necessary to
     meet them.

3   *Imagination*
     Demonstrate imaginative and innovative approaches in the
     practice of law (within the bounds of professional conduct).

4   *Workload*
     Seek additional work as necessary. Similarly, seek assistance
     if your workload is too heavy.

C   *Client relationships*

1   *Client relations*
     Ability to analyse and understand client problems quickly,
     and to display a professional and caring attitude.

2 *Client retention*
Be well-versed in client-retention skills and demonstrate the ability to manage all client-related activities effectively. (To begin with, your skills in this and the following category will be negligible. A lot may also depend on your firm's attitude and latitude. As you move towards partnership, these skills will become much more important.)

3 *Client development*
Exhibit business development skills, that is, the ability to generate additional business from existing clients and to attract new clients to the firm.

4 *Reputation*
Act in a manner that befits and best represents your firm and the legal profession at all times.

D *Professional relations*

1 *Lawyer relations*
Maintain friendly, professional relations with all lawyers, whether internally, in other firms, at the Bar, domestically or overseas.

2 *Non-legal relations*
Maintain friendly, professional relations with other advisers outside the firm, as well as with all secretaries, legal executives, paralegals and support staff, giving them the same treatment as you would other professionals.

3 *Ability to refer work*
Demonstrate the ability to refer work to both the appropriate area of expertise, as well as the lowest competent level able to handle such work. (Again, in the early days, the scope for delegation, and your ability to do it, will be negligible, but will become increasingly important as your career develops.)

4 *Dedication to the firm*
Display a strong sense of dedication and commitment to your firm, placing its goals above your own personal goals, and

contributing to its overall advancement and development. A willingness to abide by the firm's policies and procedures is also critical. In time, this will also mean contributing as appropriate to the management of the firm, and to the training and professional development of other lawyers.

E   *Personal development*
      The following qualities are also important in your longer-term development: maturity, poise, attitude, self-confidence, integrity, flexibility, and involvement in the wider business and social communities.

II   *Objective criteria*

You will have to assess your recorded chargeable hours against the target or norm set for you by the firm, as well as the extent to which your chargeable hours have been converted into fees billed to clients (do not expect either of these to be too great during your first months with the firm). There may also be some assessment of the non-chargeable hours you record. Too many firms emphasise these objective criteria at the expense of or to the detriment of the subjective criteria. Such an approach is short-term and misguided.

7.3.3   Setting goals

As an anonymous sage once said, 'Most people aim at nothing in life – and hit it with amazing accuracy'. Setting goals – the personal measure of development – and striving for them gives meaning to life. Achieving them constitutes success. These goals may be objective and overt: the trappings of wealth or power. They may be subjective and covert. They define where you want to go and how you are going to get there, and determine whether you have arrived.

Your professional activities should form part of a wider, balanced life. For this reason, any goals that you set yourself should not be restricted to your career but should look at your life in general. Success usually comes with self-confidence, and you can increase that by increasing your own competence. Knowledge and skills develop with practice, and the fear of failure correspondingly recedes with experience. Goals are the measure of your increasing competence in all things.

Choosing personal goals is not easy, but the following guidelines might help:

(a)   Goals should be personal to you, based on what you want to do rather than on what you feel you should do.

(b)   They should focus on your potential, not your limitations (both tend to be self-fulfilling, other things being equal).

(c)   Goals should be challenging, designed to stretch you and move you forward.

(d)   They should nevertheless be realistic – aim high, but not too high. If achievement is guaranteed, your goals are not challenging enough.

(e)   Finally, your goals should be specific and measurable, wherever possible setting a value or a timescale for each one.

You are likely to have a number of goals that you want to achieve. Concentrate on two or three at any one time. Plan time to achieve them and to monitor progress. The unexpected will certainly happen, so make allowances in your plans.

7.4   THE PATH TO PARTNERSHIP

The most elusive skill of all has been left until last: how do you get yourself on to the firm's notepaper? You may not be surprised to learn that there is no sure-fire way of doing it or of going about it. There is no generally accepted model statement of what it takes to be a partner; nor is there any statement of the minimum requirements for the job.

For many people, partnership is a reward offered for being a good lawyer who has been with the firm for a certain number of years. Views differ about what being 'a good lawyer' means, and the number of years can vary from two to ten. Some firms use the concepts of 'associate' and 'salaried partnership' to lengthen the period of time it takes to become a full profit-sharing (or equity) partner. This 'reward theory' of partnership is fraught with dangers, and the recession of the early 1990s serves to emphasise them.

Between them, the equity partners in a law firm are its owners. A wide range of skills, qualities and abilities is required of them collectively. Only exceptionally does a single lawyer possess all of them or even a large part of them. Yet the reward theory provides advancement to partnership on a very narrow basis – good lawyering (as yet undefined) and 'long' service. Ownership requires business generation, management and financial skills, human relationship skills, and many other things besides. It also implies risk: the risk that, in the final analysis, the profit generated by the business, and the longer-term stability of the business, may not be as secure at the next year-end as they were at the beginning. The reward theory has produced too many 'employee-minded' partners and partnerships, unwilling to take risks, unwilling to invest, unwilling to accept that incomes go down as well as up, unable to generate sufficient new work, and unable to run their practices as businesses. This description is extreme, but most firms tend to have some partners with this mentality.

The first thing to do, therefore, is rid yourself of the notion that partnership should be your reward. If it comes, partnership is a responsibility, an obligation. It carries certain privileges – to share profit, to be involved in the management and development of the firm, to contribute to the capital and overdraft – but also to share in the firm's liabilities, for instance. For a fuller explanation, see appendix 3.

In the sort of firm that most of us would want to be partners in, it is difficult to be over-prepared for partnership or to be too good for it. Take a look again at the self-appraisal criteria in 7.3.2: they provide a description of the skills and qualities most firms are looking for. Look also at appendix 3, where the role of an equity partner is described (in what some lawyers – even partners – would regard as a model statement): it shows what further qualities and attitudes may be required. If, on mature reflection, you want to be a partner, develop along these lines. They cannot guarantee you partnership, but they will make it more likely.

A final thought for you: even if you are a brilliant lawyer, a great business-winner, with many of the fine qualities that would make many a firm desperate to have you, you may still not be offered partnership in your firm. There are three reasons for this which you must not overlook, however aggrieved you may feel:

(a) the firm may not need another partner – the area in which you work may already have sufficient or too many partners;

(b) the firm may not be able to afford another partner – never overlook the financial implications for the practice that the admission of new partners will entail;

(c) there is always the 'X' factor – do the other partners like you, feel that you will make a good partner, and be happy to invite you into the inner sanctum?

Partnership is not a reward, and you cannot force any partnership to give it to you, however dedicated and meritorious your behaviour.

Good luck!

Appendix One

Specimen Reminder System Form

Client Name: _____

Client and Matter Number: |__|__|__|__|__|__| |__|__|__|__|__|__|

Department: Commercial ☐ Property ☐ Litigation ☐

Matter Partner: _____

Assigned Lawyer(s): _____

Description of Matter: _____

_____

_____

Action Required: _____

_____

_____

Deadline Date: _____

Action Date: _____

Reminder Date: _____

Submitting Lawyer: _____

Appendix Two

Phonetic Alphabet

A   Alpha
B   Bravo
C   Charlie
D   Delta
E   Echo
F   Foxtrot
G   Golf
H   Hotel
I   India
J   Juliet
K   Kilo
L   Linda
M   Mike
N   November
O   Oscar
P   Papa
Q   Quebec
R   Romeo
S   Sierra
T   Tango
U   Uniform
V   Victor
W   Whisky
X   X-ray
Y   Yankee
Z   Zulu

Appendix Three

The Role of an Equity Partner

General

Equity ownership in a law firm should be offered to a lawyer who meets the necessary business and professional criteria identified by the firm as important to it in maintaining a viable business which is responsive to clients' needs. Equity partnership is a position of trust – trust in the legal and business ability of other partners, and trust that partners will be given equitable treatment. While admission to partnership gives partners certain rights, it also imposes important responsibilities.

Accountability

Perhaps the most important element of trust amongst partners is their willingness to place the interests of the firm ahead of their individual interests, and to be accountable to other partners for both their professional and business conduct.

A partner's willingness to be accountable is evidenced in day-to-day behaviour. It includes:

(a) Accepting work for which there is the likelihood that the firm will be paid at or above the normal rates (unless any other arrangement has been approved beforehand).

(b)   Delegating wherever appropriate.

(c)   Conforming to the firm's billing procedures.

(d)   Chasing aged debts with the same energy used to represent clients.

(e)   Submitting timesheets on time.

(f)   Subscribing to and implementing the team approach to practice.

(g)   Earning your keep – not just for a few years, but until you retire, leave or otherwise alter your relationship with the firm.

Expectations

When a lawyer is invited to become a partner, it means that the other partners are demonstrating their trust in the lawyer, and that the new partner is not only a good lawyer but has many other qualities that are important to building a law firm. These qualities and characteristics are difficult to define. Further, not every partner has every characteristic, and each partner will have these qualities in varying degrees.

Partners are expected to:

(a)   Develop clients:

   (i)   Be effective in developing new business from existing clients and prospects.

   (ii)   Contribute to the business development efforts of others.

   (iii)   Develop and maintain positive relationships with clients.

   (iv)   Be available and attentive to clients.

   (v)   Have the client's confidence in your abilities and satisfaction with your work.

   (vi)   Be willing to transfer the responsibility for clients to others when appropriate.

   (vii) Handle client complaints or other quality control problems as they arise.

   (viii) Promote and cross-sell the firm's other services.

(b)   Manage your practice as a team player:

  (i)   Introduce clients to other lawyers to ensure continuity.
  (ii)   Contribute to the efficient distribution of work and client contacts.
  (iii)   Specialise and develop expertise in particular areas to complement other abilities in the firm.

(c)   Be a dependable team player:

  (i)   Be willing to put in extra hours to handle surges in workload.
  (ii)   Exhibit stability and maturity.
  (iii)   Be dependable and handle referred matters diligently.
  (iv)   Work well under pressure.
  (v)   Maintain good working relationships with partners and staff.
  (vi)   Respect each partner's professional and management judgment.
  (vii)   Comply with management procedures.
  (viii) Support the firm's objectives and treat clients as assets of the firm rather than as personal possessions.
  (ix)   Attend the firm's meetings diligently.

(d)   Work productively:

  (i)   Work efficiently and effectively.
  (ii)   Work at your level of competence, demonstrating a willingness and ability to delegate work both to the lowest competent level and to a higher level when appropriate.
  (iii)   Supervise the work you delegate.
  (iv)   Manage a reasonable workload, working independently and producing work in a timely fashion.

(e)   Produce quality work:

  (i)   Know the applicable law within your own specialised area (including current developments).
  (ii)   Handle complex client matters.

(iii) Analyse a situation quickly and accurately.
(iv) Be creative and innovative in solving client problems.
(v) Be able to plan and implement legal strategies.
(vi) Work accurately and thoroughly.
(vii) Write clearly and persuasively.
(viii) Negotiate skilfully in a client's best interests.
(ix) Be able to handle the unexpected.
(x) Exercise good judgment, differentiating between when to decide and when to consult with others.
(xi) Continue to develop professionally.

(f) Be involved in professional and community activities:

(i) Participate in professional bodies and activities.
(ii) Hold positions of leadership in community organisations.
(iii) Maintain good relationships with other lawyers and professionals in the community.

Rights

Ownership in a law firm typically brings with it the right to participate in the firm's business affairs, and in its success or failure. These rights are usually set out in the partnership agreement, and typically include:

(a) Voting on various issues.
(b) Sharing in profits and other benefits.
(c) Receiving benefits for building the firm (death, disability, retirement).
(d) Participating in management if elected or appointed.
(e) Sharing in the obligations for the firm's debts.
(f) Sharing in the remaining funds (if any) if the firm dissolves.